UNIDIR/2006/9

Bound to Cooperate

Conflict, Peace and People in Sierra Leone

Anatole Ayissi and Robin Edward Poulton
Editors

UNIDIR
United Nations Institute for Disarmament Research
Geneva, Switzerland

UNITED NATIONS

NOTE

The designations employed and the presentation of the material in this publication do not imply the expression of any opinion whatsoever on the part of the Secretariat of the United Nations concerning the legal status of any country, territory, city or area, or of its authorities, or concerning the delimitation of its frontiers or boundaries.

*

* *

The views expressed in this publication are the sole responsibility of the individual authors. They do not necessarily reflect the views or opinions of the United Nations, UNIDIR, its staff members or sponsors.

UNIDIR/2006/9

UNITED NATIONS PUBLICATION
Sales No. GV.E.06.0.12
ISBN 92-9045-183-1

The United Nations Institute for Disarmament Research (UNIDIR)—an intergovernmental organization within the United Nations—conducts research on disarmament and security. UNIDIR is based in Geneva, Switzerland, the centre for bilateral and multilateral disarmament and non-proliferation negotiations, and home of the Conference on Disarmament. The Institute explores current issues pertaining to the variety of existing and future armaments, as well as global diplomacy and local tensions and conflicts. Working with researchers, diplomats, government officials, NGOs and other institutions since 1980, UNIDIR acts as a bridge between the research community and governments. UNIDIR's activities are funded by contributions from governments and donors foundations. The Institute's web site can be found at:

www.unidir.org

CONTENTS

As the title of this book says, governments and international organizations are "bound to cooperate" with the people if they want to avoid conflict and make progress. The peace process binds political leaders to the leaders of civil society, whose voices need to be expressed. This book expresses those voices: it has been written by leaders of civil society in Sierra Leone. Not only the people of Sierra Leone, but the whole of Africa can find lessons here about building peace.

For more than a decade the United Nations Institute for Disarmament Research (UNIDIR) has been researching weapon collection and grass-roots participation. From this research it emerges clearly that peace and disarmament cannot be achieved without the active participation of civil society and civil society organizations (CSOs). CSOs are vital partners for governments and international organizations undertaking disarmament, demobilization and reintegration (DDR) and security sector reform. Without human rights organizations and strong local governance groups, security sector reform will be weaker and the abuse of power will not be curbed. Without the pressure of organized civil society, judges will be weak, police will be venal and there will be no rule of law. Without CSOs, and especially the mobilization of women, disarmament, reintegration and reconciliation cannot succeed.

UNIDIR research and the experience of UN peace operations are creating new perceptions about peace, human security and the state. Many countries have suffered from the failure of post-colonial, centralized regimes—and many have been further discredited by incompetent civil and military regimes. African traditions of decentralized, community governance were suppressed by colonial rule. Then, with the end of colonialism, young political parties repressed civil society in their efforts to build strong, new, one-party states.

But since the early 1990s, countries like Senegal and Ghana and Mali have been creating new mechanisms for decentralized governance. Decentralization strengthens civil society—not just the urban groups that are so often perceived by donors as the most important, but the rural civil society organizations of Africa: village associations and cooperatives, unions of workers and artisans, women's credit unions, youth groups and a thousand other associative networks.

This new millennium has seen civil society (including inter-faith councils, press associations and the media) become one of five pillars in the modern West African state, alongside the executive, the legislature, the security forces and the judiciary. Civil society has regained its historic African position as the second pillar, second only to the executive. In many countries, civil society is replacing a discredited legislature as the most important representative voice of the people, and supplanting the judiciary as a primary source of conflict mediation.

As our Sierra Leone case studies illustrate, civil society has become the indispensable partner in peace-building and disarmament. While peace agreements may be signed in the plush hotels of capital cities, the real work takes place in the villages, where militias hide and weapons need to be collected. No peace accord illustrates this better than that of Côte d'Ivoire: negotiations in the Parisian suburb of Marcoussis have not yet had an impact either on the rebels in the north or the *patriotes* militia in Abidjan. Perhaps we should be looking for a new approach to peace negotiation, based on the strengths of African civil society and the capacity of grass-roots and women's organizations. The chapters in this book certainly seem to point us in that direction.

The people of West Africa need to build peace more than ever and during this, UNIDIR's 25th anniversary year, we have decided to reprint these voices of civil society. This book is the result of a UNIDIR action-research partnership with West African civil society organizations to promote the Economic Community of West African States' moratorium on small arms and light weapons (SALW) that was signed in Abuja on 31 October 1998. The original edition of the book is out of print, yet people still want it because its ideas are relevant to Africa's current problems. Conflict continues to threaten Côte d'Ivoire, Guinea, Guinea-Bissau and Liberia; these countries can learn from the lessons of neighbouring Sierra Leone. Voices from Sierra Leone also need to be heard in Chad and Sudan, Uganda and as far away as Africa's Great Lakes region, where weapons, and refugees, abound.

Some of the problems raised in these chapters have yet to be settled in Sierra Leone. The corruption described by Abdulai Bayraytay is as damaging as ever: it is threatening to undermine the government of President Kabbah. Looking at Sierra Leone's governance systems today, it is painful to re-read and still recognize the descriptions by Joe Alie, Michael Foray and Abubakar Kargbo of the "failed state syndrome" and the politics of systematic exclusion that destroyed the country's state institutions. The institutional problems analysed by Nat Cole and Chris Charley are as acute now as they were when they were first written. Political protectionism remains pervasive: some Sierra Leoneans are suggesting that senior international cadres should be co-opted for the central bank, the national police, and the offices of Attorney General and Accountant General—as is the case for judges on the Sierra Leone High Court.

From the wreckage of the post-colonial state comes a ray of hope in the form of emerging alternative, decentralized governance systems. The work of civil society organizations is described in the chapters of Isaac Lappia, Michael Foray, Chris Squire and Binta Mansaray as indispensable for reconciliation and disarmament. Village councils, age groups and women's associations emerge as key players for peacemaking, with greater influence than the outside-imported institutions. CSOs offer a way forward in terms of governance.

The disarmament and demobilization process has officially ended in Sierra Leone, but the questions of rehabilitation, reconstruction and reconciliation described by Francis Kai-Kai have not all been solved. West Africa has huge numbers of under-employed young people, who need education and jobs. Education in Sierra Leone is now so run-down that teachers remain unpaid—a sign that the state is still failing. What will replace discredited education models? In the absence of massive state investment in infrastructure and job creation, civil society offers alternative paths to prosperity, and community schools are just one such innovation. Rehabilitation and reconciliation of former combatants must take place at the community level. Rebuilding roads and bridges and markets, restoring families, communities and a sense of confidence between neighbours are the stuff of peace-building. And decentralized governance appears to offer the best means of achieving all these.

Africa challenges us to seek alternative models for building peace. UNIDIR's work on this goes back to the 1994 project *Disarmament and*

Conflict Resolution—Managing Arms in Peace Processes. Since then our research on West Africa has taken us through *A Peace of Timbuktu* (where the first Flame of Peace in 1997 transformed weapon destruction into an act of public confidence-building) and the West African small arms moratorium, to *Implementing the United Nations Programme of Action on Small Arms and Light Weapons* and our current work on peace-building and disarmament with civil society in Sierra Leone and Liberia. Two years ago, a UNIDIR seminar in Geneva on participative processes and the evaluation of weapon collection, funded by the Government of Japan, confirmed the importance of establishing partnerships with civil society organizations. This book provides more evidence that civil society is an indispensable pillar of the modern African state. Thanks to Anatole Ayissi and Robin Edward Poulton for bringing together these voices. UNIDIR is also grateful for to the governments of Canada, Ghana, Sweden and the United Kingdom; without their financial help, this work would not have been possible.

Patricia Lewis
Director
UNIDIR

Africa's economic and social development has been held back by armed conflict that has inflicted death, injury, hunger, homelessness and family break-up on the innocent and deprived some of the poorest of our people of the chance of decent standards of basic human needs such as security, housing, health, education and economic prosperity. Furthermore, the aftermath of conflict has left a legacy of weapons and ammunition that fuel crime and lawlessness, thus depriving Africa of the stability it needs for economic and social development.

The Economic Community of West African States (ECOWAS) remains firm in its conviction that unchecked proliferation of small arms poses a major threat to national and regional security. This proliferation fuels conflicts, engenders increased criminality and facilitates cross-border instability. It is imperative that we get rid of these tools of death and misery.

In direct response to this situation, and recognizing the fact that our objectives for economic development can only be achieved in an environment of peace, security and stability, the Heads of State and Government of ECOWAS on 31 October 1998 signed a Declaration of a Moratorium on the Importation, Exportation and Manufacture of Small Arms and Light Weapons in West Africa.

However, for this declaration to have practical impact on the ground, we need the involvement of civil society; that is, the direct implication of those who suffer most from the scourge of small arms and light weapons proliferation. For effective and efficient action to take place on a sustainable basis, ordinary women and men from West Africa must be closely involved in the process. This people-based engagement is certainly the best guarantee for success.

Advocating for civil society involvement is one thing. Finding the right strategy for that is quite another. We should avoid ill-fated top-down approaches that dictate to people what is good for them, what needs to be done and how. Here is a good opportunity to remember that in other areas (economic and social development notably) in the past such top-down policies have not only been ineffective, but in the long run, they have ended up being counter-productive. The time is ripe to learn from past mistakes and work together toward the integration of the people of Africa in the implementation of policies that affect them.

This imperative of getting the grass roots on board is what the work of UNIDIR's project on Peace-building and Practical Disarmament in West Africa is all about. With this publication, UNIDIR gives a voice to the civil society of Sierra Leone and lets it tell what it thinks is the best way, not only to take part in the peace-building process, but also to collaborate with political authorities and the international community in our collective effort to tackle the scourge of small arms proliferation. This is a unique move as far as arms regulation and arms control policies are concerned in this region. UNIDIR has given the civil society of Sierra Leone the opportunity to contribute to the national and regional debate on the control of small arms proliferation. UNIDIR's initiative is not only timely, it also shows the way for innovative action. There is a need for sensitization campaigns in order to further mobilize West African civil society and to encourage it to initiate all necessary complementary measures that would enhance or promote policies against small arms proliferation.

We welcome this initiative from UNIDIR. It deserves our consideration and it benefits from our full support.

Lansana Kouyate
Executive Secretary
ECOWAS

ACKNOWLEDGEMENTS

UNIDIR would like to express its gratitude to the governments of Canada, Ghana, Sweden and the United Kingdom. Their generous financial contributions made this work possible.

The editors also take this opportunity to thank all those who, through their moral and intellectual support, contributed to the accomplishment of this book.

First, we express our warm gratitude to the contributors to this edited volume who have worked through the most difficult circumstances in Sierra Leone and who cared so much for the project that they continued through some of the most unspeakable violence in their country. With God's help, these women and men will have a major role to play in the great task of rebuilding a peaceful Sierra Leone. Particular thanks go to: Ibrahim ag Youssouf, consultant to UNIDIR's project on Peace-building and Practical Disarmament in West Africa; Ivor Richard Fung, Director of the United Nations Regional Centre for Peace and Disarmament in Africa, and his team in Lomé; the Bamako PCASED office; the ECOWAS Secretariat; and Brigadier Dick Bailey of the Conflict and Humanitarian Affairs Department of the United Kingdom Department for International Development.

We also want to thank: Dr Sama Banja, Minister of Foreign Affairs, Dr Kadi Sesay, Minister of Economic Development, Mrs Zainab Bangura and her team at the Campaign for Good Governance, Dr George Coleridge Taylor and Mr Edward Sams, Human Rights Commissioners, Mrs Florella Hazeley of the Inter-Faith Council, and Mr Abubakar Multi Kamara and Mrs Alison Parker of UNDP in Freetown.

Last, but not least, our thanks also go to our colleagues from UNIDIR, notably Ms Isabelle Roger, Administrative Assistant, Ms Anita Blétry, Specialized Secretary (Publications), Ms Jackie Seck, Research Programme Manager, Dr Christophe Carle, Deputy Director, and Dr Patricia Lewis,

Director. Their invaluable contributions to the realization of this work is deeply appreciated.

Anatole Ayissi and Robin Edward Poulton

ABOUT THE AUTHORS

Alie, Joe A. D., is a lecturer in history at Fourah Bay College, University of Sierra Leone and head of the Country Research Team of the African Centre for Development and Strategic Studies—a UNDP-supported policy research and strategic study project. He has done extensive research and presented papers at home and abroad on conflict and conflict management in Sierra Leone. Dr Alie is also actively involved in training leaders of community-based organizations in Sierra Leone on conflict resolution approaches.

Ayissi, Anatole, is a diplomat, specialized in disarmament matters. He is currently the West Africa Project Manager at UNIDIR.

Bayraytay, Abdulai, is a Bachelor of Arts with honours degree holder in political science from Fourah Bay College, University of Sierra Leone. He is the Information and Research Officer at the Campaign for Good Governance, a local advocacy NGO in Sierra Leone. As a practising journalist for years, he has written several articles on issues of corruption, peace and conflict resolution.

Charley, J. P. Chris, graduated with a Bachelor of Arts in Education degree in 1980. He served as a teacher at Rokel secondary school in Freetown from 1980 to 1984. He later enlisted as a cadet Assistant Superintendent of police and now holds the rank of Chief Superintendent of police. He has attended several courses at home and abroad. He has worked in different departments of the Sierra Leone Police Force including general duties, criminal investigations, traffic, immigration, special branch, prosecutions, and currently heads the research and planning department. He is married with four children.

Cole, Nat J. O., is the Director of the Customs and Excise Department in Sierra Leone.

Foray, Michael, is the Executive Director of the Movement to United People (MUP), Sierra Leone.

Kai-Kai, Francis, is a development economist. He studied at Fourah Bay College (University of Sierra Leone) where he obtained his BA (Hons) degree in 1979; proceeded to the University of Reading, United Kingdom, where he graduated with a postgraduate diploma in Agricultural Economics in 1983 and an MSc (Agricultural Economics) in 1984. In 1991–1994, he was at the University of Giessen, Germany, where he obtained his PhD degree in Agricultural Economics and Rural Development. He has worked extensively in the field of development (operations research; project design, development, implementation, monitoring and evaluation; policy analysis; etc.) over the last 18 years. He worked as Director of Resettlement, Rehabilitation and Reconstruction in the National Commission for Reconstruction, Resettlement and Rehabilitation in Sierra Leone from 1996 to 1999; and was appointed Executive Secretary in the National Committee for Disarmament, Demobilization and Reintegration (NCDDR) in September 1999.

Kargbo, Abubakar, was a lecturer in political science at Fourah Bay College, University of Sierra Leone. As a researcher, his main current areas of interest are the politics of West African integration in an era of globalization, African conflicts and resolution, and the Sierra Leone peace process. He received his MA and PhD Judr. in International Relations and International Law and Organization from Charles University in Prague, Czech Republic.

Lappia, Isaac, is the Director of Amnesty International Sierra Leone, a position he has held for three years. He has attended a series of international conferences on human rights and has organized several conferences on community disarmament initiatives to facilitate the speedy implementation of the Lomé Peace Accord signed by the Government of Sierra Leone and the Revolutionary United Front in July 1999.

Mansaray, Binta, is a Master of Arts degree holder in French. She is the Gender Desk Officer at the Campaign for Good Governance; a peace activist as well as advocate for gender equality. She is currently conducting a study on the effect of the nine-year armed conflict on women in Sierra Leone.

Poulton, Robin Edward received his history MA at St Andrews, economics MSc at Oxford (via Freetown) and his doctorate at the Ecole des Hautes

Etudes en Sciences Sociales in Paris. After 17 years working with civil society in West Africa, he is currently Senior Research Fellow at UNIDIR.

Squire, Chris, is a process engineer, educated at the University of Leeds, and currently lectures on thermodynamics at Fourah Bay College, University of Sierra Leone. His publications on Sierra Leone include *Ill-Fated Nation?* and *Agony in Sierra Leone.*

INTRODUCTION

PEACE-BUILDING AND PRACTICAL DISARMAMENT: BEYOND STATES, WITH CIVIL SOCIETY

> As it is civil society that is mostly affected by these weapons, it is the voice of civil society that should be heard above all.
>
> **Pieter J. Th. Marres**[1]

> These are strong voices, voices of dignity.
>
> **James D. Wolfensohn**[2]

> There are few limits to what civil society can achieve.
>
> **Kofi Annan**[3]

FROM A "WAR OF LIBERATION" TO A "BATTLE OF ANNIHILATION"

In March 1991 an armed conflict was ignited in Sierra Leone, becoming one of the nastiest wars the world has witnessed in the last five decades. The conflict began as a "rebel incursion" at the border between Sierra Leone and Liberia. An unknown group calling itself the Revolutionary United Front (RUF) claimed responsibility for the attacks and affirmed its determination to "save Sierra Leone from its corrupt, backward and oppressive regime".[4] But the revolution turned horribly wrong. After the first outburst of violence, the country turned from a "stable", corrupted and mismanaged state,[5] into an arena of frightening brutality, one of the great human tragedies of the twentieth century.

Young officers of the Sierra Leone army finally overthrew a government that was ill equipped to tackle the upheaval and incapable of initiating reforms or taking vigorous action. Most hoped that with the end of the inefficient government, the war would be over. Unfortunately, the government's overthrow brought an escalation of violence,[6] and Sierra Leone entered into a dark era of deep despair. What was labelled a "war of liberation" in 1991 degraded in content and ambition to the disastrous "operation no living thing" of January 1999—the armed invasion of Freetown by hysterical "nihilistic rebels".[7]

KEEPING FAITH IN PEACE

During the long years of mass violence in Sierra Leone, Africa and the international community have never stopped looking for solutions. Even though the conflict seemed intractable, the United Nations, the Organization of African Unity (OAU) and, most notably, the Economic Community of West African States (ECOWAS) remained deeply engaged at one level or another in the search for a constructive settlement of the crisis. The seeming intractability of Sierra Leone's civil war is explained partly by the proliferation of small arms and light weapons within the whole West African subregion and their financing through the illegal diamond trade. "The proliferation of small arms is a major cause in sustaining and compounding armed conflicts",[8] says OAU Secretary-General Salim Ahmed Salim. This is absolutely true in the case of Sierra Leone. Observers recognize that "national security" and "local conflicts" are no longer appropriate terms in West Africa. Conflict is a shared risk, as violence in one country spills across frontiers, where ethnic identities and refugee migrations complicate the peacemaking process. In the case of Sierra Leone, peace will not come unless and until Guinea and Liberia join the peace process. Porous frontiers must be policed on both sides. The trade in diamonds and other commodities must follow the rules of normal commerce, not the rules of the arms smugglers. Lasting peace requires that the anarchic dissemination of small arms and light weapons and ammunition in the subregion be stopped.

In November 1996 President Alpha Oumar Konaré of Mali introduced the idea of a regional moratorium on small arms.[9] The moratorium came into existence on 31 October 1998, when the ECOWAS Heads of State and Government, "considering the fact that the proliferation of light weapons constitutes a destabilizing factor for ECOWAS Member States and a threat to the peace and security of [their] people", signed a Declaration of a Moratorium on the Importation, Exportation and Manufacture of Small

Arms and Light Weapons. The moratorium, which is established for a renewable period of three years, took effect the next day.[10] For most observers, the moratorium is "a beacon of light"[11] in the particularly bleak West African security environment.

BEYOND THE STATE: BUILDING PEACE WITH CIVIL SOCIETY

A key innovation in the collective fight against small arms proliferation in West Africa is the significant role attributed to civil society by West African political authorities. This is something radically new in the African political universe, where the state has always been the primary initiator and the ultimate benefactor of security policies.[12]

From the outset, civil society was a full partner in the West African small arms moratorium. Article 4 of the Code of Conduct for the Implementation of the Moratorium states that "In order to promote and ensure coordination of concrete measures for effective implementation of the moratorium at national level, member States shall establish National Commissions, made up of representatives of the relevant authorities and civil society."

The United Nations Secretary-General, Kofi Annan, is one world leader who has recognized the important role that civil society can play in making societies better (in terms of peace, security, development and good governance). He believes that "there are few limits to what civil society can achieve". In the same vein, the World Bank mentions "civil society in all its forms" as one of the "key players" to be taken into consideration in the elaboration and the implementation of economic and social policies.[13] This is a welcome change from top-down policy-making.

A top-down approach to peacemaking and peace-building has shown its limits not only in Sierra Leone. Time and again, elegantly drafted peace agreements are signed by heads of state and heads of rebellions, only to fail because they did not carry the support of the armed fighters in the field. In Mali, the 1992 National Pact failed partly for this reason; only in 1995 did peace come, through the mobilization of civil society.[14] If we re-examine the Sierra Leonean peace process from this community-rooted perspective, it becomes apparent that this country does not need to be an "ill-fated nation".[15] Maybe the conflict looks intractable because it has been handled through exclusively "ill-fated" (top-down) strategies.

UNIDIR RESEARCH ON MICRO-DISARMAMENT AND PEACE-BUILDING IN WEST AFRICA

Seeking innovative solutions and approaches to disarmament issues is one of the tasks specified in the mandate of UNIDIR. The papers in this book have been commissioned with innovation in mind. The West African moratorium on small arms started life as a "top-down" initiative. It will become an effective tool for peace-building only if the signatures of the ECOWAS heads of state are supported by practical activities in the field. Among the authors here are key actors for implementing the moratorium: the customs service, the police, the National Commission for Disarmament, Demobilization and Reintegration (NCDDR), and a number of civil society organizations (CSO), including people working with human rights, with ex-combatants and child soldiers, with women victims, widows and women peacemakers. Each of these actors must play a role in the fight against arms proliferation. Each of our authors can provide the "alternative forms of leadership" that are needed to turn the moratorium document into practical disarmament.

The UNIDIR project on Peace-building and Practical Disarmament in West Africa encompasses a comprehensive strategy that includes both state institutions and civil society, the two sides acting in a collaborative and complementary way. It is a successor to the important UNIDIR research series that came out of the Disarmament and Conflict Resolution project, examining experiences across the world.[16]

Disarmament is (wrongly) perceived as a matter exclusively for governments and the United Nations. Ordinary people—the main victims of small arms—have to be committed to the implementation of policies aimed at curbing the proliferation of small arms and light weapons. Citizens have to be made aware that, while the decision to regulate the circulation of small arms and to implement disarmament measures may be taken by national political authorities or by the United Nations, the issue concerns their personal security, their own life and those of their children. They have a key role to play in the process of disarmament. For disarmament policies such as the moratorium to be efficiently implemented, civil society needs to be involved in the entire process from the beginning. It is the creativity of non-governmental actors that can contribute most significantly to the new thinking on peace, security and development in West Africa.

The partnership between UNIDIR and local non-governmental organizations (NGOs) has created a process in Sierra Leone and Liberia, where we are encouraging debate and discussion on security, practical disarmament and peace-building, and the role that preventing the spread of small arms must play in national and regional security. This book is an outcome of this partnership. It is a collection of papers from civil society actors in Sierra Leone, brought together to think about the meaning of peace and security and the conditions required to ensure disarmament and sustainable stability in Sierra Leone.

We are acutely aware that these debates must not be restricted to a few elite researchers. It is vital that the thinking and ideas contained within these papers reach local people, particularly the people in villages near the borders, where small arms and ammunition are transported into regions of conflict. Consequently, national and regional debates on civil society, small arms and security in West Africa will be organized around the ideas expressed in these writings, which will be widely distributed to civil society organizations, the media, political authorities and other stakeholders in the implementation of the moratorium. These debates on security, security sector reform, disarmament, arms regulation and preventive diplomacy are an important opportunity for civil society organizations to communicate their findings and recommendations to decision makers and, through the media, to the wider public within the subregion.

We see this project as "Phase One" in a much wider process, through which research is designed to feed into a long-term strategy of increasing awareness. CSOs must work at the grass roots to convince people that small arms and light weapons are a major threat to human security in West Africa. The people with whom we are working, and whom we hope to involve in the longer-term process, will be acting as:

- monitors of the West African moratorium and other disarmament, arms control and arms regulation policies;
- builders of awareness of the issues of small arms, human security and regional peace in whatever institutional frameworks may exist in the future; and

- partners of—and advisers to—the security forces for micro-disarmament and peace-building.

Not only could these UNIDIR-trained researchers and monitors be part of the national commissions for the implementation of the moratorium (recommended in Article 4 of the Code of Conduct for the Implementation of the Moratorium), they could also report nationally and internationally on progress in implementation. The local researchers and actors working with UNIDIR are closely involved in their local communities. Their work could form the beginning of an independent monitoring body for the moratorium and for future disarmament and arms regulation policies.

UNIDIR AND CIVIL SOCIETY ORGANIZATIONS WORKING IN PARTNERSHIP WITH THE GOVERNMENTAL SECTOR

Controlling the proliferation of small arms in West Africa is a complicated task, demanding a vast range of skills and a large mobilization effort in terms of human, material, political and financial resources. The plague of small arms is deeply rooted; its networks are widespread. In such circumstances, close cooperation between relevant international actors working in favour of disarmament appears the best guarantee for sustainability.

UNIDIR is presently strengthening its long-standing cooperation with its main partners in the region, notably the United Nations Development Programme (UNDP), the Executive Secretariat of ECOWAS in Abuja, Nigeria, the Department for Disarmament Affairs at the United Nations in New York and the United Nations Regional Centre for Peace and Disarmament in Africa in Lomé, Togo. This collaboration has been instrumental to the moratorium process. In fact, the idea of a West African moratorium on small arms was introduced for the first time in 1996 at a conference jointly organized by UNIDIR and UNDP in Bamako on Conflict Prevention, Disarmament and Development in West Africa. UNIDIR is also working in close collaboration with the mechanism charged with implementing the moratorium: the Programme for Coordination and Assistance for Security and Development (PCASED) based in Bamako.

The UNIDIR project is obviously only one piece of the construct. We think it is a crucial component, because UNIDIR is involving civil society in seeking complementary avenues for peace-building. This publication brings our research into the public domain; it takes the concept of partnership beyond UN institutions and donors, into the very social structures of Sierra Leone. This is not just another collection of outside "experts" talking about conflict in West Africa. These are the leaders of civil society whose work will determine whether the reintegration and rehabilitation of former fighters will really work. In enabling these writers to communicate their views, we hope to encourage a much-needed debate on security and security sector reform in West Africa.[17] We hope to enrich the understanding of Sierra Leone's partners and donors. In the long run, we believe that this partnership approach will shore up the peace builders, and contribute to sustainable peace across the whole region.

CONTENT OF THE PAPERS

The chapters of this book wrestle with fundamental questions of practical disarmament and peace-building in Sierra Leone. They were written prior to the May–June 2000 upsurge of violence in Freetown, which led to the arrest of Foday Sankoh. The violence of May–June only serves to underline the relevance of the authors' analyses.

What links this series of papers is the fact that all the authors are actors: they are Sierra Leonean civic leaders who are working for sustainable peace in their country. Each author is involved at one level or another in the search for a permanent peaceful resolution to the civil war, and a solution to the destabilizing influence of small arms and light weapons.

For the last decade, Sierra Leone has been through a series of tragedies from which complete recovery will be very difficult. **Joe A. D. Alie** presents the background to the conflict. What went wrong? Why and how? Then **Abubakar Kargbo** offers a detailed analysis of "the long road to peace". His chapter analyses the seven years of peace efforts, from the outburst of violence in March 1991 to the signing of the Lomé Peace Agreement.

When asked what their country's most fundamental problem is, Sierra Leoneans usually answer: "politics and the politicians". When asked what the problem with "politics and the politicians" is, they (and a majority of Africans) answer: "corruption". **Abdulai Bayraytay** offers a striking account of how corruption and mismanagement brought Sierra Leone to anarchy and chaos, and explains why there cannot be effective arms control and arms regulation in a deeply corrupt political environment.

On 7 July 1999, a peace agreement was signed in Lomé, officially ending war in Sierra Leone. Among other important recommendations, the agreement provides for the disarmament, demobilization and reintegration (DDR) of former combatants. The best chance for peace in Sierra Leone lies in the success of this DDR programme. Where does it stand today? **Francis Kai-Kai**, head of the national DDR programme, shows that implementation is far from healthy. This is not a good omen for the future of peace and security in post-war Sierra Leone.

As we have discussed in our strategy to involve civil society, local communities and grass-roots NGOs represent great potential for the disarmament, reintegration and reconciliation processes. **Michael Foray** focuses on this aspect of "peace by other means". Foray demonstrates that in peace-building, there is often a "missing link" in DDR programmes sponsored or led by multilateral institutions (such as the United Nations, ECOWAS, the World Bank or the European Union) and programmes undertaken by the state. The "missing link" is the community level, essentially represented by what the Carnegie Commission on Preventing Deadly Conflict calls "pivotal institutions of civil society".[18] Foray says the answers must be found in communities. In Sierra Leone, local NGOs, operating under extremely difficult circumstances, show that the neglected link to civil society may provide a powerful bridge leading to sustainable post-conflict peace and reconciliation.

A different example of "community-based disarmament" is described by **Isaac Lappia**. He shows how small, community-led disarmament initiatives were stimulated by radio announcements about the signing of the Lomé Accord. Local rebel commanders decided to discuss peacemaking with their enemies, because they and the villagers around them were glad of the chance to stop fighting and make peace. Such local initiatives, undertaken far away from the capital city—and outside UN or ECOWAS demobilization camps—can provide peace, and promise opportunities for further reconciliation in a severely fragmented society suffering from mass proliferation of weapons.

Women constitute another important component of civil society. They have a determining role to play in practical disarmament and post-conflict peace-building in Sierra Leone. How did Sierra Leonean women struggle over the past years to keep hope alive? Why did some women support the RUF, and even participate in violence, rape and mutilation? What role can women play in disarmament and arms control policies in post-conflict Sierra Leone? What are their needs and how can they be helped? These difficult questions are raised and answered in the challenging paper by **Binta Mansaray**. Mansaray sets out a list of requirements for women to be more able to participate in Sierra Leone society.

Within the context of the West African moratorium in particular, the police force and the customs service are key governmental institutions. In a post-war situation, the state strives to restore law and order through these services, especially for arms control and arms regulation. **Chris Charley**, Head of the Sierra Leone Police Research and Planning Department and **Nat J. O. Cole**, Director of the Customs and Excise Department, describe some of the problems they are facing after two decades of conscious neglect (and sometimes worse) by central government. They examine (1) the potential role for their respective institutions in the implementation of disarmament, arms control and arms regulation policies and (2) the immediate problems that will have to be overcome to play this role effectively.

Peace negotiations require compromise, which implies that all sides have to surrender important points of principle. One of the questions raised most often in discussions of the Sierra Leone peace agreement concerns the amnesty granted to Corporal Foday Sankoh and his followers. Events have moved forward since the agreement was signed: new breaches of the peace have occurred, which fall outside the amnesty, and Foday Sankoh is again in detention. Following the model of South Africa (despite a very different political context), Lomé proposed a Truth and Reconciliation Commission (TRC). Whatever post-conflict reconciliation process might be adopted by Sierra Leoneans, the "price of peace" is bound to be high. **Joe Alie** examines this "price" from his current vantage point as an adviser to the National Commission for Democracy and Human Rights (NCDHR) in Freetown. He presents the arguments for and against the amnesty, and examines the TRC. How far is "not too far" in terms of "concessions" and "sacrifices" for peace in Sierra Leone today? What balance to strike between the imperative of peace and the exigency of justice? How to transform "peace" and "justice" into non-mutually exclusive goods for post-conflict Sierra Leone? In short, how to deal with the complex challenges and the various moral and political dilemmas posed by the unspeakable crimes committed by Sierra Leoneans on other Sierra Leoneans, which still litter the road to genuine peace and reconciliation?

The current configuration of power in Sierra Leone shows that the *frères ennemis*—the government and the rebels, and also the various rebel factions—have no alternative but to cooperate (this is certainly one *raison d'être* of the Lomé Peace Agreement). On the one hand, in order to build respectability and to achieve their political ambitions, it is necessary for insurrectional forces to "get out of the bush" and cooperate with the government. On the other hand, it is equally imperative for the government to cooperate with the rebels. How to transform this mutual necessity into a constructive avenue for peace? From an analysis based on lessons learned in crisis management, power-sharing and regime-building, **Chris Squire** concludes that Sierra Leonean political rivals are "bound to cooperate", if sustainable peace is to return to the country.

CONCLUDING REMARKS

This is the first in a series of works designed to feed into the debate on sustainable peace, security and development in West Africa. The next in the series will present a collection of papers from civil society actors in Liberia. Depending on funding, we will publish similar studies by civil society in other ECOWAS countries. We hope that giving a voice to articulate ordinary women and men of West Africa will:

1. Encourage other local actors to debate the ideas expressed in these chapters.
2. Create a new impetus for research and action in the search for successful practical disarmament and peace-building.
3. Promote dialogue between politicians, government institutions and CSOs.
4. Strengthen the voice of civil society and women in debates too often dominated by soldiers and male politicians.
5. Initiate and encourage new thinking among regional and international civil society, multilateral organizations and policy makers.

6. Foster cooperative efforts to build lasting peace in a region where one nation's security is bound up in the peace and stability of its neighbours.

Anatole Ayissi and Robin Edward Poulton
Geneva
September 2000

Notes

1   Pieter J. Th. Marres (Ambassador of the Kingdom of the Netherlands to the Organization of African Unity), Address to the "International Consultation on the Illicit Proliferation, Circulation and Trafficking in Small Arms and Light Weapons", Addis Ababa, 22–23 June 2000.

2   James D. Wolfensohn (President of the World Bank), Address to the Annual Meeting of the Board of Governors, 28 September 1999, as quoted in Deepa Naraya (ed.), *Voices of the Poor. Can Anyone Hear Us?* New York: Oxford University Press for the World Bank, 2000.

3   Kofi Annan, "Secretary General Calls Partnership of NGOs, Private Sector, International Organizations and Governments", United Nations Press Release SG/SM/6973.

4   See the RUF's political manifesto: *Footpaths to Democracy. Towards a New Sierra Leone,* at <sierra-leone.org/footpaths.html>.

5   William Reno, *Corruption and State Politics in Sierra Leone,* Cambridge: Cambridge University Press, 1995.

6   I. William Zartman (ed.), *Preventive Negotiation,* Rowman & Little, 2000; I. William Zartman (ed.), *Elusive Peace. Negotiating an End to Civil Wars,* Washington, DC: Brookings Institute, 1999; Thomas C. Schelling, *Stratégie du conflit,* Paris: PUF, 1986.

7   On the devastating invasion of Freetown by the rebels in January 1999 ("operation no living thing"), see Omuru E. A. David, *The Coming of the Killers. Operation Burn Freetown,* Freetown, 1999; William Shawcross, *Deliver Us from Evil. Warlords and Peacekeepers in a World of Endless Conflict,* London: Bloomsbury, 2000, p. 283.

8   OAU Secretary-General, Salim Ahmed Salim, Address to the First Meeting of African Experts on Small Arms and Light Weapons, Addis Ababa, 17–19 May 2000.

9   The concept was presented at an international conference in Bamako on Conflict Prevention, Disarmament and Development in West Africa in November 1996. The conference was jointly sponsored by UNIDIR and UNDP. See UNDP, *Back to Basics: Post-Conflict Peace-Building in West Africa*, New York: United Nations, 1997, pp. iv–v; the idea is described as a "historic and innovative proposal calling on interested African governments to declare a moratorium on the import, export and manufacture of light weapons". See also Jacqueline Seck, *West Africa Small Arms Moratorium. High-Level Consultations on the Modalities for the Implementation of the PCASED*, Geneva: United Nations, 1999.

10   Economic Community of West African States, Declaration of a Moratorium on the Importation, Exportation and Manufacture of Small Arms and Light Weapons in West Africa, Twenty First Ordinary Session of the Authority of Heads of States and Government, Abuja, Nigeria, 30–31 October 1998. The text and background of the moratorium are presented in the second edition (in French) of UNIDIR's analysis of the Malian armed conflict and successful peace negotiations: Robin Edward Poulton and Ibrahim ag Youssouf, *La paix de Tombouctou: gestion démocratique, développement et construction africaine de la paix*, Geneva: United Nations, 1999.

11   Patricia M. Lewis, "The Future of Disarmament", in *Disarmament and Conflict Prevention in Development Cooperation*, Bonn: Bonn International Center for Conversion, 2000, p. 26.

12   On African post-colonial conflict, see Alex Thomson, *An Introduction to African Politics*, London/New York: Routledge, 2000; Bart Moore-Gilbert, *Post-Colonial Theory*, London/New York: Verso, 1997; Ato Quayson, *Postcolonialism. Theory, Practice or Process?* Cambridge: Polity Press, 2000.

13   The World Bank, *A Proposal for a Comprehensive Development Framework*, Washington, January 1999, p. 9.

14   Kare Lode (ed.), *Synthèse du processus des rencontres intercommunautaires du nord du Mali, d'août 1995 à mars 1996*, Stavanger: Misjonshogskolens forlag, 1996; République du Mali, *Livre Blanc sur le "problème du nord" du Mali*, Bamako: Imprimerie Nouvelle, 1994; Robin Edward Poulton and Ibrahim ag Youssouf, *Peace of Timbuktu: Democratic Governance, Development and African Peacemaking*, Geneva: United Nations, 1998.

15   Chris Squire, *Ill-Fated Nation?* Freetown: Ro-Marong Industries Ltd, 1995.

16 Virginia Gamba et al, *Managing Arms in Peace Processes*, Geneva: United Nations, 1998.

17 On security sector reform, see Comfort Ero, *Sierra Leone's Security Complex*, London: Centre for Defence Studies, 2000; Dylan Hendrickson, *A Review of Security Sector Reform*, London: Centre for Defence Studies, 1999; United Kingdom Department for International Development (DfID), *Security Sector Reform and the Management of Military Expenditure: High Risks for Donors, High Returns for Development*, London: DfID, June 2000.

18 Carnegie Commission on Preventing Deadly Conflicts, *Preventing Deadly Conflicts*, New York: Carnegie Corporation of New York, 1997, p. 109.

CHAPTER 1

BACKGROUND TO THE CONFLICT (1961–1991): WHAT WENT WRONG AND WHY?

Joe A. D. Alie

SIERRA LEONE: THE MAKING OF A TRAGEDY

In March 1991 an obscure rebel movement calling itself the Revolutionary United Front (RUF), led by an ex-corporal of the Sierra Leone Army, Foday Sankoh, launched a series of guerrilla attacks on border towns in eastern Sierra Leone. Their first operation was an attack on the police station at Bomaru in Kailahun District on the Sierra Leone–Liberia border. During the encounter, the RUF succeeded in over-running the station and capturing most of the weapons there. The RUF aimed to overthrow the All People's Congress (APC) party government headed by Major-General Joseph Saidu Momoh, whose administration the RUF described as corrupt, inefficient, tribalistic and lacking popular mandate. The government did not take the attack on Bomaru Police Station seriously; it was interpreted as a small skirmish over trading transactions between some irresponsible elements from the Liberian and Sierra Leonean border guards. Some APC politicians even argued, if less convincingly, that the skirmish was orchestrated by some unpatriotic opposition elements in the southern and eastern regions of Sierra Leone who were bent on derailing the democratic process that was unfolding after a long period of one-party rule. In short, rather than grapple with the issue directly, the political leadership sought simplistic interpretations and advanced conspiracy theories to address what later turned out to be a very complex and thorny problem.

It should be recalled that a few months earlier, Charles Taylor (leader of the rebel National Patriotic Front of Liberia—NPFL) had, in a British Broadcasting Corporation (BBC) programme, threatened to punish Sierra Leoneans for allowing their territory to be used as a base for the Economic Community of West African States Monitoring Group's (ECOMOG) peacekeeping operations against his movement. In Charles Taylor's words, "Sierra Leoneans would taste the bitterness of war" because of their support for ECOMOG. In his view, ECOMOG's presence in both Sierra Leone and Liberia prevented him from shooting his way to power in Liberia. Tom Woewiyu, spokesperson for the NPFL, argued: "Sierra Leone's participation in ECOMOG was the chief factor in the NPFL's problems. You cannot be peacemakers and still fight us at the same time." It is important to note that Foday Sankoh's RUF invaded Sierra Leone from territory controlled by the NPFL. Moreover, the RUF forces initially comprised many mercenaries provided by Charles Taylor. But Taylor had more reasons for supporting the RUF. He wanted unlimited access to the rich agricultural and diamondiferous lands in south-eastern Sierra Leone, in order to pay for his elaborate war machine in Liberia.[1]

In the absence of a coordinated strategy by government forces to contain the situation, the RUF rebels, with considerable logistics and other forms of support from Charles Taylor and other West African leaders, began slowly to advance northward and westward. In the process their ranks swelled with recruits, many through abductions. By 1992 the RUF had become a force to reckon with.

Since the RUF invasion of 1991, Sierra Leoneans have been struggling with a macabre war. This war brought into sharp focus the serious political problems that had confronted the nation since the attainment of political independence in 1961. It set in motion brutal and cruel forces that have engulfed the entire country in an unprecedented civil conflict. This conflict, in the words of Abdul Karim Koroma, "brought into graphic relief that side of human nature which, given appropriate circumstances, can be transformed from good to evil, graciousness to brutishness, sharing and caring to a display of primeval instincts".[2] The war has left in its wake mass destruction of lives, property, settlements and unprecedented violations of human rights. It has also rendered the government incapable of meeting its social, economic and other responsibilities to the citizens, as the state economy has been totally depleted.

Given the particularly brutal nature of the war, a cursory analysis could easily lead to the conclusion of a senseless and inexplicable rebel insurgency. However, a deeper analysis of the underlying causes of the war would invariably lead to a trail that links its escalation to the country's long-term economic and social decline as well as a prolonged history of social injustice.

WHAT WENT WRONG AND WHY

The war has changed society and Sierra Leone will hardly be the same again. Sierra Leoneans, therefore, need to ask themselves certain painful questions.

- What went wrong? How and when did it go wrong? Is it something that just happened with the arrival of Charles Taylor, or were the seeds of the problem planted a long time ago, and Foday Sankoh was simply there to harvest their fruits?
- What would have happened if Sierra Leoneans had had unity of purpose?
- What would have happened if there were justice, fair play and sufficient opportunities and equality of opportunity; if there were less selfishness and more responsibility on the part of the elite; if there were more protection of society from external and divisive situations?
- What would have happened if Sierra Leone were a more cohesive society?
- Would the war have followed such a violent course if there had not been disempowerment of the rural populations through a deliberate destruction of decentralized governance and the corruption of state institutions by the centralized one-party system of Siaka Stevens?[3]

Honest answers to these questions would, in our view, lead to a better understanding of the roots of the civil conflict.

OVERCENTRALIZATION OF STATE MACHINERY

Sierra Leone inherited from the British, in 1961, the promise of a budding democracy. There was a functioning parliamentary system exercising legislative power in an elected house of representatives, while executive power resided in a cabinet headed by the prime minister. Judicial power was in the domain of an independent court system that had the Supreme Court at the apex. Other arms of government, such as the civil service, army and the police had highly qualified and motivated personnel who were respected for their industry, loyalty and commitment to duty. The nation's educational institutions were the envy of sub-Saharan Africa.

Local government bodies, popularly elected by the people, performed useful functions and were mainly responsible for development at community and chiefdom levels. Politicians were in close touch with their constituents and regularly explained government policies and plans to the people. They, in turn, took back messages and grievances from their constituents to government. Thus, there was regular and fruitful communication between the rulers and the ruled. If the people perceived that their elected representatives were not working in their best interests, they had an opportunity to replace these representatives in regular and transparent elections. This was demonstrated, for example, during the general elections of March 1967 in which the opposition All People's Congress (APC) defeated the ruling Sierra Leone People's Party (SLPP), thereby becoming the first opposition party in post-colonial Africa to oust a ruling party through the ballot box.

Unfortunately, the APC abandoned its previous (1961–1967) commitment to participatory democracy: after 1967 the country was dominated by a single-party dictatorship that created an environment of bad governance. The APC instituted a highly centralized, inefficient and corrupt bureaucratic system of government, marginalizing the people and robbing them of their rights and freedoms. Henceforward policy acquired a national character only when it originated from State House.

As early as 1970 some members of the APC noticed that the Prime Minister and leader of their party, Siaka Stevens, was beginning to display autocratic tendencies. As a result, two of his close associates, Dr M. S. Forna and Mr M. O. Bash-Taqi, Ministers of Finance and of Development, respectively, resigned their membership of the APC and proceeded to form a new party with Dr John Karefa-Smart (another leading politician in the country) and others—the United Democratic Party (UDP). In his letter of resignation to the Prime Minister, Bash-Taqi wrote: "It gives me greater pain to see that you have embarked on a road of rapid destruction of those high ideals and fundamental principles for which we fought so vehemently over the last years." Dr Forna in like manner described Stevens as the "evil spirit behind the use of force and violence" and referred to "a display of infantile vanity and manifestations of a megalomaniac syndrome".

The bulk of UDP support came mainly from Freetown and the Northern Province, and particularly from the Temne. The split within the APC was more than a storm in an African calabash. It was a major threat to Siaka Stevens, whose greatest appeal throughout his political career had been to the Freetown community and to the Temne and allied groups, such as the Limba (whereas the SLPP's main political base was further south among the Mende).

Siaka Stevens, armed with emergency powers, quickly proscribed the UDP, arguing that it was an ethnic-based party bent on destabilizing the country. The party was also accused of being financed by foreign interests. The UDP's followers reacted with violence, staging attacks on APC offices and other government targets in the Northern Province and in Freetown.

The violence was brutally suppressed, the UDP and its newspaper banned, and its leaders jailed. Some fled the country. Meanwhile, the APC-dominated Parliament had been making dramatic moves to transform the country into a republic. This controversial action was completed on 19 March 1971. Two days later Siaka Stevens made himself Executive President with wide powers. On 23 March Force Commander John Bangura and other officers were arrested for a coup plot. They were subsequently executed. A relative of John Bangura, Foday Sankoh, who was a corporal and photographer in the army, was also implicated in this coup plot and jailed. It is this same Foday Sankoh who reappeared as the leader of the rebel war on 23 March 1991—exactly twenty years after his arrest for involvement in the Bangura coup plot.[4]

The concentration of power in the hands of a few people in the capital made access to resources impossible for non-APC members. Thus, membership of the APC became a necessary condition to get by. The excessive centralization of public administration weakened local government structures, thereby robbing the development process of the active participation of the greater part of the population at the grass-roots level. Local government bodies such as Rural Area Councils, District Councils and Chiefdom Councils became dysfunctional. Where they existed, they merely served the interests of the party-government, because the members of these councils were not popularly elected, but appointed by Freetown. As a result the specific needs, realities and circumstances of the provincial and rural communities were either marginally treated or, in extreme circumstances, neglected outright. Even simple extractive functions like local tax collection were controlled from the centre.

Overcentralization accelerated the crumbling of the fabric of the state and finally led to state collapse.[5] State collapse meant complete loss of control over the political and economic space: the government was in no way able to generate enough revenue to provide adequate services for its citizens; and neighbouring rogue states were able to encroach on Sierra Leone's sovereignty by directly involving themselves in its politics and by hosting dissident movements. A feeling of disenchantment set in.

RURAL ISOLATION

Visible evidence of overcentralization was the lack of equity in resource allocation, leading over the years to a feeling of deprivation and alienation by the rural folk. These areas were almost completely cut off from the centre and government influence in the rural areas was, at best, minimal. Socio-economic "development" was confined to Freetown and a few other towns. But the money used for such development was obtained mainly from the rural masses through agricultural and other activities. This led rural Sierra Leoneans near the Liberian border increasingly to identify themselves with Monrovia (capital of Liberia) rather than with Freetown. Government workers in remote parts of the country, such as teachers, frequently went for months without pay, and these articulate groups became very bitter against "the system". This encouraged them to assume confrontational positions in crisis periods. Youths and young adults in particular perceived officials in the capital as working against their interests (both individual and collective).

Growing poverty and isolation in the countryside contributed significantly to rural–urban migration, with its accompanying problems. Many rural migrants were unable to find jobs in the city and so drifted into idleness and destitution. They became potential participants in mob action. In this way overcentralization in Africa creates the conditions for mob action and revolt.

Those who remained in the rural areas did not seem to know or care much about what was happening in the capital city; nor did the city residents know what was happening in other parts of the country. For a long time the rebel war was viewed largely as a provincial affair, which had little to do with the capital.

FACTIONALISM AND ETHNIC POLITICS

Sierra Leone, like many other African states, is a multi-ethnic society. Some 17 ethnic groups collectively occupy a geographical area of 27,925 square miles. The two largest groups are the Temne, who occupy large sections of the Northern Province, and the Mende, who dominate the southern and eastern parts of the country. Together, Mende and Temne account for roughly 60 per cent of the country's population. They have, over the years, influenced culturally and otherwise other ethnic groups within their domain.

The Mende and Temne have been dominant players in the political life of Sierra Leone before and since independence, and political leaders from both groups have often appealed to their kith and kin for support. Sometimes intense competition for political power has led to major conflict. This was particularly evident during the first decade of independence, 1961–1970. Other important players in the national political arena have been the Krio (who inhabit the Western Area), the Limba (sometimes dominant in the APC) and the Kono, whose homeland in the far east of Sierra Leone is rich in diamonds.

During most of the post-colonial history of Sierra Leone the two big political parties have been the Sierra Leone People's Party (SLPP) and the All People's Congress (APC). Although the SLPP, which ruled the country 1961–1967, drew its followers from every part of the country, it was largely perceived by opposition elements—and even by certain non-Mende SLPP party stalwarts—as a party representing mainly the interests of the Mende and those with close affinity to the Mende. To the Northerners and particularly the Temne, the SLPP leadership did not seem to pay much attention to regional balance in power-sharing arrangements. Some Northern politicians complained, for example, when Prime Minister Sir Milton Margai (a Mende) effected a cabinet reshuffle shortly before independence that the Temne felt denied them some important positions in the government. John Cartwright observed:

> Unease among Northerners, particularly Temnes, had been growing
> slowly as Sierra Leoneans assumed a greater share of power in the

government. Sir Milton (the Prime Minister and leader of the SLPP) had taken steps to allay Temne fears in 1957 by appointing Kandeh Bureh and I. B. Taylor-Kamara as well as his close supporter Dr Karefa-Smart to important portfolios, and later added Y. D. Sesay and Paramount Chief Bai Koblo to the Cabinet, but in 1960 this concern for balance seemed to lessen. The Temne leaders in the SLPP hoped in 1960 for the appointment of one of their number to the newly-created post of Deputy Prime Minister "to bring peace between the two tribes", but instead the position went to (M. S.) Mustapha, an Aku Creole. A further blow to Temne pride came with the announcement of new... United Front Ministers; the Mendes received one additional post, the Creoles three, but the Temne none. Two of the newly-created appointments were carved out of Temnes' ministries, which appeared to many Temnes to be further indication that they were being downgraded.[6]

In the midst of this political turmoil, in October 1960, the APC was born. Its leader was Siaka Stevens, a Limba, though born in the southern town of Moyamba. The APC attracted a large following from the North. Many Northern politicians gravitated toward the APC and encouraged their countrymen and women to join the party, believing it was the only party that would genuinely seek their interests. They blamed the SLPP for the apparent backwardness of the North. Some Northern politicians even suggested that their new party be called "Northern People's Party", but Siaka Stevens opposed this. However, the APC leadership at the time of the party's inception consisted solely of two major ethnic groups from the North—Temne and Limba. The principal leaders were Siaka Stevens (Leader, Limba, trade unionist and politician); C. A. Kamara-Taylor (Secretary-General, Limba and transport owner); S. A. Fofana (Temne, tailor); S. I. Koroma (Temne, transport owner); M. O. Bash-Taqi (Temne, politician); Prince Koh (Limba, politician).[7]

The APC party appeared desperate to lead the country: their motto, for instance, was "Now or Never". It received considerable support from the Krio and the Kono, probably because these groups felt that they would not be able to make much headway in the SLPP. Although the leadership of the APC may have been prepared to use constitutional means to achieve its objectives, the rank and file felt otherwise. Some APC members attempted to wreak havoc during the 1961 independence celebrations in Freetown by violence and sabotage. While the celebrations were largely peaceful, explosions occurred at Freetown's main power stations. Telephone lines between Freetown and the provinces were cut, and an unsuccessful attempt was made to sabotage a major bridge in Freetown. The government was forced to declare a state of emergency. Following the declaration of a state of emergency, APC leaders were arrested and detained during the independence celebrations. Certain SLPP supporters in Freetown (who were predominantly Mende) decided to counter APC violence by forming a militia called the United Front Volunteers—although they did not engage in any acts of violence. The APC leaders were released shortly afterward.

In the first general elections after independence in 1962, the APC and their allies secured 20 seats, the SLPP 28, independent candidates 14 and paramount chiefs 12. Most of the APC seats were won in the North and the Western Area (Freetown and its environs). The APC thus emerged as the official opposition in Parliament.

It is important to note that the disparity in socio-economic development between the North and South, which certain Northern politicians alluded to in order to garner support for their cause, was not a deliberate policy of the SLPP government. It was a colonial legacy. During the colonial period most of the government's economic activities had been concentrated in the South and East, where the main cash crops (coffee, cocoa) were grown to satisfy demand in Europe. The South and East also had rich deposits of strategic minerals, including diamonds. The Southerners appear to have embraced Western education much more vigorously than the Northerners, who were pro-Muslim. The early and sustained exposure of the Southerners to Western influences gave them an edge over other provincial groups in the post-colonial politics and administration of the country.

It can be argued, however, that certain Northern politicians blinded themselves to economic realities. While Northerners lacked natural resources, they adequately compensated for it in commerce, for they controlled most of the retail trade in the country. Islam arrived in West Africa through trade and has retained this commercial tradition.

Politically, it would seem that the country was polarizing along ethnic or sectional lines. The situation became worse after 1964 when Sir Milton Margai died. He was succeeded by his brother Albert Margai (although some in the SLPP felt that a non-Mende in the person of either the "darling of the North", Dr John Karefa-Smart, or M. S. Mustapha should have succeeded Sir Milton). Albert Margai took immediate steps to punish four non-Mende ministers who had criticized his appointment by the Governor-General. They were M. S. Mustapha (a Krio), John Karefa-Smart and Y. D. Sesay (North), and S. L. Matturi (East). Their dismissal from the government was a mistake, causing further political tension, for these were influential people who represented important areas in the country.

Albert Margai's subsequent actions may have aggravated the already tense ethnic situation in the country. For example, he advised provincial chiefs to discourage APC activities in their chiefdoms, and the national broadcasting service was instructed not to publicize the APC. An absenteeism bill was rushed through Parliament in May 1965, which stipulated that any Member of Parliament who absented himself from parliament for 30 consecutive days "without reasonable excuse" would lose his seat. As a result, four APC parliamentarians, who were in jail on convictions of riot and assault, lost their seats. Not surprisingly, the APC would later use similar legislation (in 1977) to deprive four SLPP parliamentarians of their seats: one of these was Sir Albert Margai's son, Charles (subsequently serving in 1999–2000 as Interior Minister). Charles Margai and others had been detained on various charges, including murder, after the 1977 general elections. They were released soon after losing their seats.

Albert Margai (who later became Sir Albert) was also accused of "Mendenizing" the civil service and the army. Certain Mende (or people with close affinity with the Mende) had been appointed to senior positions. John Kallon (Mende) was Establishment Secretary, Peter Tucker (Sherbro) was Secretary to the Prime Minister, S. B. Daramy (Mandingo) was Financial Secretary, while David Lansana (Gola) was promoted to the rank of Brigadier and made head of the army. In terms of qualifications and experience, however, these people merited their positions.

The polarization of the country along ethnic/regional lines was also creeping into the army. While it was widely believed that Brigadier-General David Lansana supported the Prime Minister, his Deputy Colonel, John Bangura (a Northerner), was sympathetic to the APC. Shortly before the general elections of March 1967 Bangura and some other officers were implicated in a coup plot. And even though the officers arrested included three Southerners, the arrest, particularly of the Krio and Northern officers, was seen as a last, desperate attempt by Sir Albert Margai to complete his mastery over the army in preparation for the forthcoming elections. This gave the APC a propaganda tool to appeal to both Krio and Northern solidarity.[8]

The elections went ahead as planned but they exposed once again the dangerous levels of ethnic tension in the country. The APC won all the seats in the North but one, all contested seats in the Western Area and some in Kono District, while the SLPP won almost all seats in the South and most seats in Kenema and Kailahun and Kono Districts. The final results were APC 32 seats, SLPP 28, and independents 6. The Governor-General proposed that the leaders of the SLPP and APC form a government of national unity, but attempts failed when the head of the army, Brigadier-General David Lansana, staged the first successful coup in the country's post-independence history. Lansana advanced many reasons for taking over the government. He said, for example, that the elections had been fought on an ethnic basis, a situation that could lead to civil war. But other officers felt otherwise. They believed that the Brigadier intended to reappoint Sir Albert Margai as Prime Minister. A group of colonels arrested both the Brigadier and Sir Albert Margai, and took over government themselves.

Following the restoration of constitutional rule through a counter-coup by junior officers loyal to the APC in April 1968, Siaka Stevens returned from exile in Guinea and was appointed Prime Minister. He lost no time in replacing Mende officers in the army with Northerners. In May 1969 John Bangura was promoted to Brigadier-General and Force Commander. When Siaka Stevens later fell out with Bangura, he appointed another Northerner—Joseph Momoh, a Limba—to the position of Force Commander.

In an attempt to consolidate their power, the APC leaders introduced a series of electoral petitions against SLPP supporters, which the latter lost. The APC—perhaps because it was now visibly in power or because the elections were characterized by violence and intimidation—won the ensuing by-elections, thereby substantially increasing its representation in parliament.

The years 1968–1970 were particularly difficult for the SLPP and the Mende community generally, including those in Freetown. The Mende were being punished for the sins of the SLPP as if the party had comprised only Mende. In the east end of Freetown, at Ginger Hall, where there was a large concentration of Mende, APC thugs beat up people suspected of being SLPP and set fire to houses belonging to SLPP supporters. In reaction, most Mende living in the South and East of the country firmly resolved not to have any dealings with the APC.

The regionalization of national politics led to a series of bloody clashes between supporters of the APC and those of the SLPP, especially in SLPP strongholds like Bo, Pujehun, Kenema and Kailahun. During election periods, and especially in 1973 and 1977, the APC, assured of victory in the North through the infamous "unopposed system", mobilized truckloads of thugs from the Northern areas and transported them to the South and East to harass and intimidate SLPP supporters. One of the worst clashes occurred on 3 May 1977 in the Southern provincial town of Bo, a traditional SLPP stronghold. APC leaders in the town brought in several hundred youths from the North to terrorize SLPP supporters. The clash that ensued left many dead and the homes of Northerners in Bo completely destroyed. This intense rivalry between Mende and Temne for political power has had serious implications for national unity and cohesion. It has been suggested that tribalism destroyed the social fabric of the Sierra Leone society; that this was common knowledge, but that people felt it was too sensitive to discuss.

While ethnicity or regionalism may not have been a significant factor in the early stages of the civil war in Sierra Leone, subsequent events tend to support the view that it is a powerful undercurrent and needs to be properly addressed. For instance, when RUF rebels attacked a Northern town in early May 1997, a prominent Northern politician was quoted as saying that the rebels killed everybody in the town except one woman, who spoke Mende. Ethnic and regional factors could also partly explain why the RUF began operations in Sierra Leone from Kailahun and Pujehun: not only were these places close to the Liberian border, the RUF leadership probably convinced itself that Kailahun and Pujehun, traditionally safe SLPP areas, would support any movement that aimed to get rid of the APC. Nonetheless, it is instructive to note that Foday Sankoh, leader of the RUF, is a Temne, but many of his fighters are Mende. This composition is important and is perhaps a blessing in disguise for the country: it has prevented the rebel war from degenerating into a purely tribal conflict.

THE POLITICS OF SYSTEMATIC EXCLUSION

From 1968 on, there was little provision for alternative views in national politics: one was either with the ruling party or against it. Loyalty to the APC replaced loyalty to the country. This was perhaps most vividly expressed in the armed forces, where enlistment was through the recommendation of a government minister or a party heavyweight.

In 1978 all semblance of multi-party competition was eliminated by the introduction of a one-party state. Sierra Leoneans felt disenfranchised. Political leaders now established clientelist relations with potentially powerful groups like the intellectual community, the armed forces and the labour unions to maintain power. The judiciary too was corrupted and miscarriages of justice became common. Honest and hard-working Sierra Leoneans who did not favour the APC were sidelined, which seriously affected morale, especially in the civil service.

Opposition supporters were denied a fair share of the country's resources. This denial included access to jobs. Civil servants were not spared: there were many instances of illegal dismissals and sidelining of those senior civil servants who were "not in line". "Connectocracy", rather than meritocracy, became the sine qua non for advancement in the civil service and government parastatals. Those groups or regions that were perceived to be anti-ruling party were subjected to harassment and intimidation. This forced some opposition elements to go underground and wait for the right opportunity to vent their spleen on their oppressors. Excessive use of force against the opposition and suspected opposition supporters bred a culture of silence.

Siaka Stevens's supporters argued that a one-party system of government was the only practical way to eliminate political violence, which some people believed was inherent in the multi-party system. This, of course, was an illusion. The first elections under a one-party state in 1982 were accompanied by violence and intimidation on an unprecedented scale. Indeed, the aftermath of the mayhem in some areas was so great that its consequences were still being felt several years later. In the wake of the 1982 general elections, some citizens in Pujehun District formed a guerrilla movement, the Ndorgborwusui, to protect themselves against what they called "state-sponsored terrorism". Is it any wonder that the RUF attempted to recruit young men from Pujehun in the early days of the movement's existence?

CHIEFDOM-LEVEL POLITICS

Politics at the chiefdom level, especially among the ruling houses, has been characterized by intense competition since the colonial era, when the idea was first developed for paramount chiefs to sit in Parliament.[9] There were instances when the colonial administration openly supported a candidate who did not seem to command the respect of the majority of the chiefdom people. Such chiefs held their position at the pleasure of their masters and not on any traditional principle of acceptance by their people. This eroded traditional rules of reciprocity: many chiefs were able to maltreat their subjects because they knew they had the backing of the colonial government. Interference by the central administration in the politics of the chiefdoms continued after independence and sometimes created volatile situations, which occasionally resulted in violent conflicts in the chiefdoms.

Maladministration by other chiefdom authorities, such as excessive fines by Court Chairmen, created bad blood between these authorities and the young men. There were occasions when some youths had to flee their village settlements because of their inability to pay huge court fines. Such young men had the desire to take revenge on their oppressors. The RUF leadership may well have capitalized on some of these deep-seated grudges to sell their movement to certain disaffected people.

The erosion of local governance had a particular impact on weapons of violence. Under the Chiefdom Council Act, firearms permits were issued during the 1960s and 1970s by police authorities on the recommendation of village headmen and the local chief. In practice this meant that local notables were vouching for the good character of hunters; they were guarantors for the proper use of firearms in the community. This partnership between communal elders and the police broke down under the one-party system. Firearms legislation was no longer applied after the dissolution of chiefdom councils. Firearms began to circulate more freely, especially in areas close to the Liberian frontier: for the Liberian rules regarding gun ownership (inspired by American legislation) made firearms more readily available across the frontier. The growing availability of firearms would come to haunt Sierra Leone.

WEALTH, CORRUPTION AND ABUSE OF POWER

In terms of natural resources, Sierra Leone is among the richest countries in the world. As the then British High Commissioner to Sierra Leone, Peter Penfold, observed at the Consultative Conference on the Peace Process in Sierra Leone in April 1999:

> The tragedy of Sierra Leone is that her people are among the poorest in the world, while the country is among the richest. The reasons for this are entirely man-made. Other countries in the world are poor because of natural disasters, few resources, unfertile territory, or bulging populations. Not so in Sierra Leone. God blessed this land with an abundance of resources. Just a relatively few people are responsible for the misery and hardship suffered by so many.

Over the past three decades, a small minority of Sierra Leoneans have become fabulously rich and insensitive to the plight of the masses. They paraded around in expensive cars and sent their children to school overseas, while their wives and mistresses went shopping overseas. Corruption and mismanagement were rife. These vices became institutionalized in Sierra Leone from the 1970s, when the APC began to make increasing use of the patronage system to reward the party faithful. Siaka Stevens openly supported corruption as he himself acquired a great deal of wealth. He is quoted as having said that *"usai yu tai kaw, na dae i dae it"* (meaning "a cow grazes where it is tethered"). This expression more or less gave a free hand to all those who had access to public money to steal as they liked. Funds allocated for general development invariably found their way into the pockets of private individuals. From 1981 certain ministers and public officials were implicated in a series of financial scandals variously dubbed "voucher-gate", "million-gate" and "squander-gate". But little attempt was made to punish these offenders. Successor regimes also tolerated a high degree of corruption. Transparency and accountability vanished from the public administration system.[10]

Government financial management was appalling. Expenditure always ran much higher than planned. A case in point was the hosting of the Organization of African Unity (OAU) Summit in Freetown in 1980. The government ended up spending some 200 million leones (about US$ 200 million), although 100 million leones had been earmarked for the conference. No one was forced to explain what happened to the extra money.

Corruption and mismanagement affected the country in diverse ways. Governments failed to translate the country's rich mineral, marine and agricultural resources into improved welfare for the majority of the population. According to Abdullah, the economic downturn in the early 1980s, partly fuelled by the lavish hosting of the 1980 OAU Summit and by dwindling mining revenues exacerbated by rampant smuggling, affected expenditure on health and other social services. Scholarships to students also declined. He goes on:

> For the 1974/75 fiscal year, the expenditure on education totalled 15.6 per cent of government expenditure; this was reduced to 8.5 per cent in the 1988/89 fiscal year. Similarly, expenditure on health and housing dropped from 6.6 per cent and 4.8 per cent in the same period to about 2.9 per cent and 0.3 per cent, respectively. Since the State was the largest employer of labour, the downward economic trend affected the general employment situation. Thus whereas the number of pupils in secondary schools registered a phenomenal increase from 16,414 in 1969 to 96,709 in 1990, there were only about 60,000 in paid employment by 1985. By 1990, it had become impossible even for university graduates to secure jobs in the public sector, and this at a time when the private sector was downsizing.[11]

The increasing incidence of poverty led to poor sanitation and low nutritional health standards, as well as literacy rates that are among the lowest in the world. As far back as 1983, Sierra Leone was classified by the United Nations as the least developed country in the world: and since that time the country has held on to this sad position at the bottom of Africa's league table.[12]

From April 1968 until March 1992, when the APC was overthrown by young military officers, the party leadership was preoccupied with amassing wealth while maintaining itself in power at all costs.[13] People said they had changed their party motto from "Now or Never" to "Live for Ever". This meant that the party would continue to bulldoze its way to power regardless of the wishes of the people. Young people in particular point to past political failures, nepotism, and mismanagement of the country's vast resources as some of the principal causes of the rebel war.

NEGLECT AND MISUSE OF YOUTH

No group suffered more from political and economic exclusion than the under-twenties. The progressive deterioration of the economy over the years had its most adverse effect on youth. A group of young men and women, including school leavers, university graduates and ghetto dwellers emerged without jobs or any reliable means of income. For these young people life was an uphill task; they felt dejected, cut off from the mainstream of society. Losing faith in the system, some became radical and rebellious. Youth radicalism and anger against "the system" was particularly marked in the late 1970s and 1980s, when there was an urgent desire for change. Young people in Sierra Leone and elsewhere found comfort and inspiration in songs such as "System Dread", "Send Another Moses", and other lyrics by singers such as Bob Marley and Peter Tosh.

Libyan leader Colonel Qadhafi's *Green Book*[14] was another source of inspiration. This was widely read by students in Sierra Leone and its revolutionary ideas greatly appealed to them. The *Green Book* (which a former American president described as a watermelon: green on the outside, but red inside) gave many disaffected young people (including those living in the ghettos) revolutionary impetus for their crusade against what they considered an unjust system.[15] Some of the educated young men who pioneered the RUF movement were disciples of the *Green Book* philosophy. The RUF's manifesto, *Footpaths to Democracy: Towards a New Sierra Leone*,[16] is perhaps a stepchild of the *Green Book*. Many jobless young people joined the RUF when it was formed because it promised them hope, power and a new meaning in life.

Often these youths did not hesitate to vent their spleen against the establishment. For instance, at the Annual Convocation for the Conferment of Degrees at Fourah Bay College (the country's oldest university) on 27 January 1977, students staged a peaceful anti-government demonstration in full view of President Siaka Stevens, Chancellor of the university. The students called, among other things, for improved social and economic conditions and free and fair elections. APC thugs countered by staging a pro-government demonstration two days later. They attacked Fourah Bay College, committed violence and other criminal acts against lecturers and students, and damaged a lot of property. The authorities closed the college, but Freetown primary and secondary school pupils and other youths in solidarity with the college students declared "No College,

No School". They went on the rampage and soon provincial pupils joined in nationwide anti-government demonstrations. There were serious disturbances across the country. The vandalism was directed mainly against APC ministers and their stalwarts.[17] The government reacted by shutting down all educational institutions in the country.

Students staged another demonstration on 12 January 1984, which coincided with the official opening of the Eighth APC National Delegates Conference, held at the City Hall in Freetown. The students were calling for major economic reform. Unemployed youths took advantage of the situation to embark on wide-scale looting and destruction of property. ("Unemployed" may be the wrong adjective, since some, though equally marginalized, were nevertheless part of the "system"; some were employed—drugged and used by the government to suppress opposition.) Fourah Bay College was again closed for eight weeks following the disturbances (the author was then Secretary-General of the National Union of Sierra Leone Students).

Students were not alone in manifesting their discontent. On 1 September 1981 the Sierra Leone Labour Congress had initiated a nationwide strike to press for economic reform. The strike had a huge impact and the government used high-handed tactics to put down the strike. Many Congress officials were rounded up and taken to Pademba Road prison. *The Tablet* newspaper, which for some years had embarrassed Siaka Stevens's government with its incisive comments and exposés, was forced to go underground. Its editor fled the country.

LAPSES IN STATE SECURITY

Between 1961 and 1991 there was a continuing and dramatic decline in national security, resulting from politicization of the military and the police, the creation of security organizations with personal or political allegiances, rampant corruption and military coups. This seriously undermined the national security apparatus, to the extent that the RUF was able to cross the border from Liberia in March 1991 with about 100 men, and by 1995 had pursued its offensive almost as far as Freetown.

The army inherited from the British in 1961 was relatively small, well trained, professional and disciplined. Gradually, however, political interference began to creep into the process of recruiting and promoting officers. This led to a lowering of standards and morale. In 1974 the head of the army was appointed to parliament and to the Cabinet. As a result, the army lost its national character and its commitment to the national interest and national security. By 1978 recruitment into the army became commercialized, as each leading politician was allocated a share of vacancies for enlisted men. The army was consequently filled with thugs and misfits who could disobey their commanders with impunity. The soldiers, including the Force Commander, had shifted their loyalty from the state to their godfather politicians.

At the same time, the army top brass enriched themselves at the expense of the state. Officers carted away huge sums of money, leaving the soldiers poorly equipped. The rank and file of the army were disgruntled and demoralized. When the rebel war broke out, there were not even trucks to carry troops to the battlefield. Many of the disaffected soldiers went on to collaborate with the RUF rebels, to the bitter disappointment of civilians.

Despite the building of clientelist relationships, as early as 1970 Siaka Stevens had begun to lose confidence in the army. This was due partly to its propensity for staging coups. To neutralize the army, Stevens created a new paramilitary force, the Internal Security Unit (or ISU, and later Special Security Division). This force was well trained and well armed, fiercely loyal to Stevens and the APC, and was used as an anti-riot outfit to control civil unrest and student disturbances. Members of the force became so trigger-happy that they were nicknamed "ISU", to mean "I shoot you". They struck terror in the civil populace.

The police force was corrupted like the army. The Inspector-General of Police also became a Nominated Member of Parliament: thus he became a politician rather than the chief sheriff. This undermined the neutrality of the force. With the introduction of a one-party system of government in 1978, recruitment and promotion were influenced mainly by loyalty to the APC. Many recruits did not meet the basic requirements for entry into the force; they were accepted anyway. Corruption was rife, due in part to low police pay, poor accommodation, illiteracy and ignorance of the mission of the police force. Many people joined simply to get rich.

The cumulative result was that the force was unable to perform and there was a complete breakdown of security, particularly in provincial areas. For instance, under the very nose of the Intelligence Unit of the police force, Libya was sponsoring candidates and organizations in the mid-1980s to engage in illegal activities in the country. Without police detection, Foday Sankoh and student activists traversed the length and breadth of the country recruiting young men for military training in Benghazi, Libya.

The cumulative effects of all of the above factors led, in the words of the Sierra Leonean president, Ahmad Tejan Kabbah:

> ... to a culture of ... non-cooperation with the (political) authorities ... The intimidation of the general public by successive dictatorial regimes, the high level of illiteracy ... high unemployment, poverty, lack of social programmes for the youth and the failure of the judicial system killed loyalty and any sense of belonging to the State. All these created a deep-seated cynical attitude towards government, politics, politicians and the public administration apparatus.

CONCLUSION

In conclusion, this background to Sierra Leone's descent into anarchy and chaos shows that the root causes of the years of civil violence could be found in:

- Political injustice, manipulation of elections, ethnic politics, disruption of the rule of law, and the political corruption of the principal institutions of the state, notably the courts, the police, and the military.
- Mismanagement of resources and economic corruption, misappropriation and embezzlement of state funds; these were compounded by lack of accountability and transparency in the management of state resources.
- Social injustice stemming partly from political injustice and partly from economic injustice; this led to the marginalization of whole groups like the youth and the rural poor, who were to become recruits for armed rebellion.

- Overcentralization of state powers and state resources led to the total neglect of the vast majority of the population, the total collapse of local governance and the erosion of chieftain authority, deliberately engineered by Siaka Stevens.
- Mass poverty and mass illiteracy, with a growing culture of violence. The fact that these same factors were present in Liberia (where the violence actually started) shows that in our region, "conflict is a shared risk".[18]

Notes

1   For a graphic account of the civil war in Liberia and how Liberian violence "percolated" in Sierra Leone, see James Youboty, *Liberian Civil War. A Graphic Account*, Philadelphia: Parkside Impressions Enterprises, 1993.

2   Abdul Karim Koroma, *Sierra Leone: The Agony of a Nation*, Freetown, 1996.

3   See William Reno, *Corruption and State Politics in Sierra Leone*, Cambridge: Cambridge University Press, 1995.

4   Joe A. D. Alie, *A New History of Sierra Leone*, London: Macmillan, 1990.

5   On the phenomenon of "state collapse", see I. William Zartman (ed.), *Collapsed States: The Disintegration and Restoration of Legitimate Authority*, Boulder, CO: Lynne Rienner Publishers, 1995.

6   John R. Cartwright, *Politics in Sierra Leone 1947–67*, Toronto: University of Toronto Press, 1970, pp. 125–126.

7   C. P. Foray, "The Road to One-Party State: The Sierra Leone Experience", Africanus Horton Memorial Lecture delivered at the Centre of African Studies, University of Edinburgh, 9 September 1988.

8   Joe A. D. Alie, op. cit.

9   In Sierra Leone, provision has been made in the constitution (since the mid-1950s) for 12 paramount chiefs to be elected to Parliament during general elections that are normally held every five years. Each of the 12 chiefs represents one district in the provinces. The districts are as follows: (1) Northern Province: Bombali, Kambia, Koinadugu, Port Loko, and Tonkolili; (2) Southern Province: Bo, Bonthe, Moyamba and Pujehun; (3) Eastern Province: Kailahun, Kenema and Kono. One important thing to know is that the chiefs are not elected on a party

basis, that is, they do not represent political parties but the interests of their districts. They are indirectly elected through an electoral college comprising councillors and other paramount chiefs in the district. They are therefore a specific group in Parliament. However, the elected chiefs are expected to support the government of the day. Thus any political party that forms the government can always rely on the chiefs to substantially increase its voting powers in Parliament. For additional information on this topic, see Joe A. D. Alie, op. cit.

10 William Reno, op. cit.

11 Ibrahim Abdullah, "Bush Path to Destruction: The Origin and Character of the Revolutionary United Front/Sierra Leone", *Journal of Modern African Studies*, Vol. 36, No. 2, 1998, pp. 203–235.

12 See UNDP, *Human Development Report 2000*, New York: Oxford University Press, 2000; World Bank, *Entering the 21st Century. World Development Report 1999/2000,* New York: Oxford University Press, 2000; Robert D. Kaplan, "Sierra Leone: From Graham Greene to Thomas Malthus", in *The Ends of the Earth. A Journey to the Frontiers of Anarchy*, New York: Vintage Books, 1997.

13 Fred M. Hayward and Jimmy Kandeh, "Perspectives on twenty-five years of elections in Sierra Leone", in Fred Hayward (ed.), *Elections in Independent Africa*, Boulder, CO: Westview Press, 1987.

14 For more on Qadhafi's *Green Book*, see <en.wikipedia.org/wiki/The_Green_Book>.

15 I. Abdullah, op. cit.

16 Revolutionary United Front/Sierra Leone, *Footpaths to Democracy: Towards a New Sierra Leone, manifesto of the Revolutionary United Front of Sierra Leone*, 1995. Can also be found at <sierra-leone.org/footpaths.html>.

17 C. P. Foray, op. cit.

18 John B. Laggah, Joe A. D. Alie and R. S. V. Wright, "Countries in Conflict: Sierra Leone", in Adebayo Adedeji (ed.), *Comprehending and Mastering African Conflicts—The Search for Sustainable Peace and Good Governance*, London: Zed Books, 1999.

CHAPTER 2

THE LONG ROAD TO PEACE: 1991–1997

Abubakar Kargbo

MAKING WAR AND TALKING PEACE

Since the beginning of the civil war in Sierra Leone in 1991, various regimes and the international community have attempted to bring an end to the war. When the war started, the All People's Congress (APC) was in power under the leadership of President Joseph Saidu Momoh. It was taken unawares, and the government did not make any significant move to end the war, either on the battlefield or at the negotiating table. In the end, the war caused the overthrow of the APC regime by the army under the National Provisional Ruling Council (NPRC).

When the NPRC came to power on 29 April 1992, it took a bold step to end the civil war. In his address to the members of the diplomatic and consular corps in Sierra Leone on 5 January 1996, Chairman Valentine Strasser observed that there was a link between peace in Sierra Leone and in Liberia. He said that one of the factional leaders in the war in Liberia commanded strong influence over the Sierra Leonean rebels of the Revolutionary United Front (RUF). He added that the NPRC government was ready to establish contact with any Liberian factional leader, in an effort to reach a negotiated settlement of the crisis in Sierra Leone.

Additionally, in a letter addressed to the United Nations Secretary-General, the NPRC government requested the good offices of the UN Secretary-General to bring the government and the RUF to the negotiating table, with the UN serving as a mediator.[1] The NPRC government contacted the UN in accordance with the decision taken by a Paramount Chiefs' Conference in July 1994, which had been convened by the NPRC regime. The conference, among other things, called for (1) the creation of a National Security Council to initiate ways and means to bring the rebel conflict to an end and start the difficult process of reconstructing the economy and restoring democratic governance, and (2) the adoption of strategies that would form the basis for a request for assistance to the outside world.

In response, the United Nations sent an official from its Department of Political Affairs, Mr Felix Mosha, to Sierra Leone. This UN Special Envoy came to Sierra Leone to discuss with the RUF/SL (Revolutionary United Front of Sierra Leone) whether it would accept the UN as an intermediary in the dispute. The UN stressed its neutrality and insisted on the fact that its role was only that of a facilitator for the peace process. The efforts of the UN Special Envoy were in vain, however; he was not able to establish contact with the RUF/SL.

The United Nations then appointed Berham Dinka, who collaborated with the Organization of African Unity (OAU), the Commonwealth Secretariat, the Economic Community of West African States (ECOWAS) and other organizations interested in a peaceful resolution of the conflict in Sierra Leone. Berham Dinka also sought and received assistance from official bodies, private individuals and non-governmental organizations. Despite the initial impasse that characterized UN efforts to make contact with the RUF/SL, the ice was broken at the end of 1995. Ambassador Dinka met with representatives of the RUF/SL leadership in Côte d'Ivoire on 5–6 December 1995.

Meanwhile, there was a change of regime in Sierra Leone. As the result of a palace coup, Brigadier Julius Maada Bio took power from Captain Valentine Strasser as head of the NPRC government. Successful contact was made with the RUF leadership. This meeting gave hope for a peaceful settlement, because this was the first time the RUF leadership had met and held talks over the conflict in Sierra Leone with an officially designated organ. Since there can be no lasting peace without participatory democracy and good governance, the United Nations was also instrumental in promoting the democratization process in Sierra Leone, which led to the holding of elections and the formation of a government under the leadership of President Ahmad Tejan Kabbah and the Sierra Leone People's Party (SLPP) on 29 March 1996.

THE ABIDJAN PEACE ACCORD AND THE AFRC *COUP D'ÉTAT*

Two months later, the SLPP government met with the RUF in Yamoussoukro (May 1996). In his attempts to find a peaceful resolution to the conflict, the UN Special Representative attended the Yamoussoukro talks. Although the talks failed, they represented an initial positive step, since the RUF leader had agreed to come to talk peace.

And Yamoussoukro led to further diplomatic activity. On 30 November 1996, the Abidjan Peace Accord was signed between the Government of Sierra Leone and the RUF. The SLPP Government of National Unity saw the signing of the Abidjan Peace Accord as a first step in the restoration of total peace in Sierra Leone.

There were initial attempts by the SLPP government to implement the accord. A National Commission for the Consolidation of Peace was established. The Commission did not, however, get off the ground. The 700 troops meant as a Neutral Monitoring Group, as proposed by the accord, were unacceptable to the RUF. Instead, the RUF proposed only 120 monitors. Meanwhile, despite the accord, attacks on civilians continued. The SLPP government blamed the RUF for the attacks across Sierra Leone, while the RUF blamed the government forces, including its Civil Defence Forces, the Kamajors.

The post-Abidjan situation was characterized by claims and counter claims on the part of both the Sierra Leone government and the RUF. The implementation of the Abidjan Accord became even more difficult when the Sierra Leone government welcomed the RUF palace coup of Fayia Musa and Philip Palmer, who declared that they had overthrown the RUF leader, Foday Sankoh.[2] The palace coup was welcomed by many Sierra Leoneans in the context of a rebel war that was by then almost six years old. They cited the willingness of the RUF under Captain Philip Palmer to reach an agreement with the SLPP Government of National Unity with a view to putting into effect the Abidjan Accord, which, four months after signing, had yet to be implemented.[3] The RUF leader, Corporal Foday Sankoh, unsurprisingly interpreted the palace coup as a conspiracy against himself and his movement.[4] A tense climate of mistrust and suspicion followed and violence escalated. When RUF rebels took Fayia Musa and others hostage, the government issued a seven-day ultimatum demanding their release.[5] Foday Sankoh ignored Freetown while he consolidated his position in the rebel movement. Needless to say, this had a devastating effect on the peace process.

It was in this troubled context that a section of the national armed forces, led by young officers, overthrew the democratically elected regime of President Ahmad Tejan Kabbah. On 25 May 1997, an Armed Forces Revolutionary Council (AFRC) was formed with Major Johnny Paul Koroma as the chairman. The AFRC was soon composed of members of the Sierra Leone Army (SLA) and the RUF, which Koroma invited to join his junta (to the horror and dismay of the citizens of Freetown). This coup coincided with the Organization of African Unity Foreign Ministers Summit in Harare. The meeting strongly condemned the coup. The then OAU chairman, President Robert Mugabe of Zimbabwe, went further, and expressed support for what he termed the noble mission of ECOWAS in Sierra Leone. The AFRC had taken power while Sierra Leone was hosting a military base for the ECOWAS Monitoring Group (ECOMOG). ECOMOG's mandate envisaged not only the restoration of peace in Liberia, but continued peace and stability in Sierra Leone and the subregion as a whole. In view of the ECOMOG mandate, Sierra Leone's government called on ECOWAS to reverse the AFRC coup. ECOWAS accepted the challenge.

The ECOWAS initiative was also strongly supported by the UN Security Council, when it met with the ECOWAS Committee of Four (charged with the management of the Sierra Leone crisis). The Security Council declared the AFRC coup unacceptable and called for the immediate and unconditional restoration of constitutional order in Sierra Leone. Meanwhile, the francophone members of ECOWAS, in their meeting of 24 June 1997 in Lomé, endorsed the ECOWAS plan to reverse the coup and restore constitutional order.

At its Foreign Ministers meeting of 26 June 1997, the ECOWAS Committee of Four was enlarged to five members: comprising Côte d'Ivoire, Ghana, Guinea, Liberia and Nigeria. In the Final Communiqué of this meeting, the Committee of Five adopted dialogue, embargo and sanctions as recommended options for the restoration of constitutional order in Sierra Leone. The possible use of force was retained in case the above-mentioned tracks failed to yield the desired result.

At the 3789th meeting of the UN Security Council, the Committee informed the Council's members of ECOWAS's determination to restore legality in Sierra Leone. The Committee received full support from the Security Council, which also supported the decision of the Thirty third OAU Summit Meeting at Harare in June 1997. The OAU Summit, among other things, underlined the need to implement the Abidjan Agreement, which was to serve as the framework for peace, stability and reconciliation in Sierra Leone.

Despite initial failures, the AFRC met the Committee of Five in Abidjan. Both parties agreed to the following points:

- The early reinstatement of constitutional order.
- The release of RUF's leader, Foday Sankoh (who was imprisoned in Nigeria).
- The implementation of the Abidjan Peace Accord.
- Amnesty for the putschists.

The agreement was not implemented, however, because of the lack of political will on both sides.

On 23 October 1997 the AFRC and the Committee of Five met again in Conakry. Here the main conclusions of the meeting were as follows:

- The military junta would in principle step down after six months.
- The release and offer of a package of opportunities to Foday Sankoh.
- Indemnity to all AFRC members and supporters.
- Disarmament and award of scholarships to AFRC members.
- A ceasefire between ECOMOG and AFRC.
- The delivery of humanitarian assistance to the civilian population.

Again, and for the same reason (lack of political will), the agreement was not implemented. ECOMOG therefore felt forced to intervene militarily, and the largely Nigerian force was successful in restoring to power the democratically elected government of President Tejan Kabbah. The AFRC retreated into the bush, quickly breaking up into its component parts as disorganized marauding bands of SLA and RUF troops.

THE REVIVAL OF THE PEACE PROCESS

On 6 January 1999, rebels of the RUF and the AFRC invaded Freetown. The invasion is remembered as one of the bloodiest episodes in Sierra Leone's nine years of war.

The mayhem of 6 January led Sierra Leoneans strongly to advocate for peace. The war had destroyed much of the fabric of Sierra Leonean society. This destructive frenzy constituted strong justification of the belief that, unless sustainable peace was attained, Sierra Leone would continue heading straight for the abyss. Sierra Leoneans called on President Ahmad Tejan Kabbah and his government to act immediately and firmly.

Despite the obduracy of the RUF and AFRC fighters, every energy was spent to attain peace for the destitute and traumatized people of Sierra Leone. Popular agitation for peace reached a peak at the very moment that the government in Sierra Leone was being criticized for its weak handling of the Civil Defence Forces, particularly the Kamajors, who were noted for their military power in the south-eastern part of Sierra Leone. There was also criticism of the state of the national police force:[6] the police force had been a particular target during the RUF attacks of January 1999, losing more than 200 men. President Kabbah's government was also accused of not supplying arms and ammunition to its armed forces unless there was a serious security setback. Against this background, many Sierra Leoneans were posing questions as to the ability and commitment of the government of Sierra Leone to safeguarding the lives and property of its people.[7]

Given the stalemate on the battlefield, it was argued that—despite its military efforts to end the war—the government must pursue the diplomatic option. For most. Sierra Leoneans, dialogue continued to be a possible option for constructive peace.

In fact, Sierra Leone's government and President Ahmad Tejan Kabbah never ruled out a peaceful settlement to the conflict. In his Address to the Nation on 21 February 1999, President Kabbah reminded all those who advocated dialogue and the need for a political settlement that while the RUF and its allies were trying to reduce Freetown to ashes, and while they were mutilating the survivors of their deadly invasion, the president of Sierra Leone had taken one of the greatest risks of his presidency by initiating a dialogue with the rebel leader, Foday Sankoh.[8]

The first turning-point toward real peace talks with the RUF happened when the government announced that it had responded to the request to allow the RUF leader to meet face-to-face with the dissident members of the RUF leadership. This was a major step on the part of the government toward lasting peace. The aim was to afford the RUF leadership the chance to come up with a plan as to how they intended to pursue the peace process.[9]

In the quest for peace, President Kabbah visited four capitals in the West African subregion: Abidjan, Abuja, Accra and Lomé. The peace process was reviewed, including prospects for an internal dialogue among the RUF/SL.[10]

Meanwhile, just a few weeks after the invasion of Freetown, the new United Nations Special Representative, Ambassador Francis Okelo, was instrumental in initiating a peace process. Meeting in Abuja with the Nigerian leader, President Abdulsalam Abubakar, Ambassador Okelo informed him that he was urging the Sierra Leone government to meet with the rebels for peace talks. The UN Special Representative also met with the RUF in Abidjan and informed its leaders of his intention to revive the peace process.

The Parliament of Sierra Leone held talks with President Kabbah. The president presented the Members of Parliament with his new peace plan for Sierra Leone. Finally, protracted diplomatic contact between the government and the RUF started in Togo on 25 May 1999.

This new beginning of negotiations took place thanks to three preconditions:

1. A document called the "National Consensus on the Road to Peace", agreed during the National Consultative Conference of April 1999.
2. Joint RUF and AFRC internal consultations.
3. The 18 May 1999 Ceasefire Declaration in Lomé, which came into effect one day before the beginning of the Lomé Peace Talks.

At last, armed with the consensus of civil society in Sierra Leone, the Sierra Leone government entered into negotiations with the rebels. The Lomé talks were carried out under the auspices of the then ECOWAS chairman, President Gnassingbé Eyadéma of Togo. The peace talks lasted 44 days. They were characterized at the beginning by accusations and counter-accusations. The RUF also made demands on the government that were unacceptable. The talks were protracted and on several occasions there was a threat that they would end in fiasco and disarray. The presence of members of the international community (the UN and the OAU, the United States, the United Kingdom) interested in a peaceful resolution of the crisis in Sierra Leone exerted pressure on both parties to arrive at a negotiated settlement.

The peace talks almost became bogged down over a number of points. Among the most difficult were the issues of power-sharing, ministerial appointments, the status of the RUF leader, the issue of amnesty, and the future role of ECOMOG in a post-war Sierra Leone.[11]

THE LOMÉ PEACE AGREEMENT

Finally, on 7 July 1999, a Peace Agreement between the Government of Sierra Leone and the Revolutionary United Front of Sierra Leone was signed in Lomé. The agreement is a comprehensive document dealing with socio-economic, security and political issues. Above all the document is legally binding on both sides. It contains a preamble and 37 articles divided into 8 parts (see Table 1). In addition there are five annexes:

I. The Agreement on a Ceasefire in Sierra Leone
II. The Definition of Ceasefire Violations
III. The Statement by the Government of Sierra Leone and the Revolutionary United Front of Sierra Leone on the Release of Prisoners of War and Non-Combatants
IV. The Statement by the Government of Sierra Leone and the Revolutionary United Front of Sierra Leone on the Delivery of Humanitarian Assistance in Sierra Leone
V. A draft schedule of implementation of the Peace Agreement

The agreement is most commonly referred to as the Lomé Accord. This document is both comprehensive and challenging. It deals not only with controversial issues like "Pardon and Amnesty" (Article IX), but it covers all the areas crucial to the long-term socio-economic and political development of Sierra Leone, as well as humanitarian questions.

Table 1: The Lomé Peace Agreement: A Synopsis

Parts	Articles	
1. Cessation of Hostilities	I.	Ceasefire
	II.	Ceasefire Monitoring
2. Governance	III.	Transformation of RUF/SL into a Political Party
	IV.	Enabling Members of the RUF/SL to Hold Public Office
	V.	Enabling the RUF/SL to Join a Broad-Based Government of National Unity through Cabinet Appointment
	VI.	Commission for the Consolidation of Peace
	VII.	Commission for the Management of Strategic Resources, National Reconstruction and Development
	VIII.	Council of Elders and Religious Leaders
3. Other Political Issues	IX.	Pardon and Amnesty
	X.	Review of the Present Constitution
	XI.	Elections
	XII.	National Electoral Commission
4. Post-Conflict Military and Security Issues	XIII.	Transformation and New Mandate of ECOMOG
	XIV.	New Mandate of UNOMSIL
	XV.	Security Guarantees for Peace Monitors
	XVI.	Encampment, Disarmament, Demobilization and Reintegration
	XVII.	Restructuring of the Sierra Leone Armed Forces
	XVIII.	Withdrawal of Mercenaries
	XIX.	Notification to Joint Monitoring Commission
	XX.	Notification to Military Commands

Parts	Articles
5. Humanitarian, Human Rights and Socio-Economic Issues	XXI. Release of Prisoners and Abductees XXII. Refugees and Displaced Persons XXIII. Guarantee of Displaced Persons and Refugees XXIV. Guarantee and Promotion of Human Rights XXV. Human Rights Commission XXVI. Human Rights Violations XXVII. Humanitarian Relief XXVIII. Post-War Rehabilitation and Reconstruction XXIX. Special Fund for War Victims XXX. Child Combatants XXXI. Education and Health
6. Implementation of the Agreement	XXXII. Joint Implementation Committee XXXIII. Request for International Involvement
7. Moral Guarantors and International Support	XXXIV. Moral Guarantors XXXV. International Support
8. Final provisions	XXXVI. Registration and Publication XXXVII. Entry into Force

THE TRUTH AND RECONCILIATION COMMISSION

One important point that has provoked heated debate among the people of Sierra Leone is the Truth and Reconciliation Commission (TRC). Central to any genuine peace process is reconciliation. There can be no sustainable peace in a severely war-torn society without reconciliation. Reconciliation usually requires truth about what happened, and an understanding of why it happened.

Article XXVI of the Lomé Peace Agreement specifically deals with this issue. It proposes the establishment of a TRC, which will be responsible for addressing issues of impunity. The TRC will break the cycle of violence and provide a forum for both the victims and perpetrators of human rights violations to tell their story. The TRC will seek a clear picture of the past, in order to facilitate genuine healing and reconciliation. In the spirit of reconciliation the TRC will be asked to consider the question of human rights violations since the beginning of the conflict in Sierra Leone in 1991.

Perhaps, in order to fully understand the nature of the TRC in Sierra Leone, we must relate it to Article IX of the Lomé Accord, which deals with pardon and amnesty. This article grants absolute and free pardon not only to the leaders of the RUF and AFRC and ex-SLA, but to all combatants and collaborators with respect to anything done by them in pursuit of their objectives up to the time of the signing of the Lomé Agreement on 7 July 1999. The implication is that no official or judicial action will be taken against any member of the RUF, AFRC, ex-SLA or Civil Defence Forces for crimes committed between 1991 and 7 July 1999. The immunity includes exiles and other persons residing outside Sierra Leone, and also assumes the full exercise of their civil and political rights, with a view to their reintegration within the framework of full legality.

On 22 February 2000, the Sierra Leone Parliament enacted The Truth and Reconciliation Commission Act, 2000.

CONCLUSION

A realistic assessment of the Lomé Accord will reveal a fine document that is an embodiment of reconciliation in Sierra Leone. No one can ignore the argument that the Lomé Accord has been seen as an imposition. Some people argue that the RUF/SL, ex-AFRC and ex-SLA should not have been given the privileged position accorded them in the Lomé Peace Agreement: that it is as if they were now being compensated for the atrocities they have committed, thus giving credence to the culture of impunity.

It has to be emphasized that the Lomé Accord is a realistic document, based on political expediency. No military victory is possible for either side. Each side believes that it has a "just cause". The agreement contains articles that underscore the absolute necessity for good governance in post-war Sierra Leone. Good governance not only enhances the peace process, it is also one of the most efficient tools for peaceful conflict resolution. The agreement creates the avenue for a more open, pluralist and participatory political order and the development of effective, transparent, accountable and responsive institutions of governance.

If promptly and faithfully implemented, the Lomé Peace Agreement will undoubtedly open a new era for participative and non-exclusionary politics in Sierra Leone. For that reason, the agreement appears to be a good recipe for sustainable peace, since bad governance is at the heart of the last nine years of anarchy and chaos in Sierra Leone.

Notes

1   *Report of the UN Secretary-General on the Situation in Sierra Leone*, New York, 21 November 1995.
2   *Week End Independent Observer*, Freetown, 17 October 1998, p. 1.
3   *AFRO Times*, Freetown, Vol. 6, No. 16, 26 March 1997, pp. 1 and 6.
4   *For di People*, Freetown, 17 October 1998, p. 4.
5   *EXPO Times*, Freetown, Vol. 2, No. 26, 19 April 1997, p. 1.
6   *Unity Now*, Freetown, Vol. 1, No. 3, 5 February 1999, p. 2.
7   *Concord Times*, Freetown, 18 March 1999, p. 3.
8   *The Democrat*, Freetown, Vol. 4, No. 2, 23 February 1999, p. 2.
9   *The Vision*, Freetown, 25 February 1999, p. 2.
10 *Herald Guardian*, Freetown, Vol. 3, No. 21, 18 March 1999, p. 3.
11 *Independent Observer*, Freetown, No. 369, 28 June 1999, p. 1.

CHAPTER 3

BOUND TO COOPERATE: PEACEMAKING AND POWER-SHARING IN SIERRA LEONE

Chris Squire

> When you slip and fall, do not look for the cause of your
> fall where you lie; the cause is where you slipped.
>
> A Mende proverb

The current power configuration in Sierra Leone should convince all aspirants to positions of leadership in the country that the politics of exclusion based on the forceful seizure of power are not viable. The government and insurgency groups never had any alternative but to cooperate. Proof, if any were needed, is that the war in the country dragged on for almost a decade without any military solution. The warring factions remain strong enough to continue to fight and destroy, but none is strong enough to win a clear and definitive "victory" over its "enemies."

Because of their action or inaction during this period of endless fighting and wanton violence, all sides have to accept responsibility for the horrors visited on the country. The Lomé Peace Agreement is a tacit acknowledgement of these realities.[1] Aspirants to positions of leadership, and indeed the country as a whole, must now contend with the following issues:

- on the one hand, if any of the insurrectional forces are to operate under any cloak of respectability and achieve their political ambitions within the context of a sane exercise of political power, *cooperation with the government is imperative;*

- on the other hand, government(s) failed to achieve a military solution to the nine-year rebel war, despite many public pronouncements that such a victory was realistic. This made the country ungovernable. If sustainable peace is to be achieved, *it is a logical imperative for the government to cooperate with the rebels*;
- by the same token, different rebel leaders are obliged to engage in "instrumental" coalitions (the Revolutionary United Front/the Armed Forces Revolutionary Council/the Sierra Leone Army, for example) in order to interface efficiently with the government and attract "legitimacy", support and sympathy from the international community.

These inherent advantages of cooperation may have provided the contending forces with the necessary preconditions for signing the Lomé Accord, but the agreement will be inadequate for ensuring sustainable peace without a demonstrated commitment from all sides to play the political game by the rules.

The question thus becomes *how does the country transform the mutually binding necessity "to cooperate" into a constructive avenue for peace?* It is this that is explored in this chapter.

THE THEATRE OF THE CIVIL CONFLICT: DESCENT INTO CHAOS

In most cases, armed uprisings are considered only in a "zero-sum game"[2] context; the main aim is the direct and outright overthrow of the incumbent government and the exclusive seizure of sovereign power. For a variety of reasons, the insurgents may not have the capacity for direct assault on the seat of power. In the case of Sierra Leone, the main rebel movement, the Revolutionary United Front (RUF), did not have the capacity for a direct, armed assault to overthrow the government. Consequently the armed rebellion has outlived four governments:

- The Joseph Momoh All People's Congress (APC): 1985–April 1992.
- The Valentine Strasser National Provisional Ruling Council (NPRC): April 1992–January 1996.
- The Julius Maada Bio NPRC government: January 1996–March 1996.

- The Ahmad Tejan Kabbah SLPP government: March 1996 to date.[3]

THE MOMOH APC GOVERNMENT AND THE "UNHOLY ALLIANCE"

In his search for a staging post to invade Liberia, Charles Taylor visited Sierra Leone in 1989, and reportedly contacted and gave money to senior members in the Momoh APC government as an incentive for granting him permission to operate from Sierra Leonean soil. After accepting his money, the story goes, officials refused to grant Taylor his request. Attempts to force the issue led to Taylor being briefly jailed in Freetown. Subsequently he was released and thrown out of the country. Later, Momoh was to allow Sierra Leone to be used as a base for ECOMOG (Economic Community of West African States Monitoring Group), which intervened in Liberia's civil war: this choice was made without any provision for securing Sierra Leone against reprisal attacks from an enraged Charles Taylor—who was to become the most powerful warlord in Liberia.

Sierra Leone has a long and undefended border with Liberia. As far as the security and the defence of Sierra Leone were concerned, the Sierra Leone Army (SLA) was useless for any significant military action. The SLA suffered from three structural weaknesses: it was politicized, underequipped and undertrained. These facts would have been known by Sierra Leonean and ECOMOG authorities, and probably by the Liberians as well. Securing the country's borders with Liberia should have been an integral part of strategic military planning for the ECOMOG incursion into Liberia, if Sierra Leone was to be the launch pad for such operations. Surprisingly, this was not the case.

When armed guerrillas dispatched by Charles Taylor crossed the eastern and southern borders of Sierra Leone in March 1991, the government reacted by recruiting new soldiers at breakneck speed, including many urban youths disenchanted with corrupt political leaders. The composition of the army, whose professionalism had for years been undermined by a recruitment policy based on clientelism, was further complicated. Momoh's government then failed to provide the troops with adequate logistics support. And yet, the government never gave any serious consideration to negotiating with the rebels.

THE DEADLY MESSIAHS: THE RISE AND DEMISE
OF THE NATIONAL PROVISIONAL RULING COUNCIL

On 29 April 1992, young military officers toppled Momoh's regime. Twenty seven-year-old Captain Valentine Strasser emerged as the chairman of the National Provisional Ruling Council (NPRC). Strasser made a radio broadcast saying what all Sierra Leoneans knew to be true: that for twenty-four years "we have been ruled by an oppressive, corrupt, exploitative, and tribalistic bunch of crooks under the APC Government". Sierra Leoneans were jubilant at the appearance of the NPRC. Every middle-aged politician who had ever promised them positive change had let them down. People felt the youth deserved a chance to put an end to the culture of official corruption. Once more the country was at a crossroads. Could the youth deliver where their elders had failed?

They started well enough: the NPRC corrected the frequent blackouts, non-payment of salaries, and attended to other social institutions and infrastructure projects. But the military regime also ushered in a period of anarchy. When the young leaders in Freetown failed to set a standard of honesty, there was no controlling their soldiers in the field, who turned to looting towns and villages. Instead of cracking down on indiscipline, the NPRC blamed the atrocities on the Revolutionary United Front (RUF). While the RUF was certainly guilty of its own share of attacks against civilians, government troops were no less involved.

Sierra Leoneans were loath to accept that the regime that had toppled the hated APC could have collapsed into anarchy. The situation remained unclear for many people until early 1994. Civilians had found themselves at the receiving end of atrocities perpetrated by the RUF. They hoped for protection from the NPRC military government and the army, an institution that is constitutionally sworn to protect their rights. The NPRC had proclaimed themselves "messiahs": they had seized power from the failed APC government and would bring peace to the country. Yet the people suffered increasingly from the raids, rapes and pillage of the rebels. Children were kidnapped. Life in certain areas of the country became hellish. The mounting evidence was that some of these self-proclaimed NPRC messiahs were part and parcel of Sierra Leone's hell on earth.

DESPERATELY SEARCHING FOR HELP: BACK TO THE SPIRITS

In desperation, a hounded and defenceless civil populace fell back on its traditions. Traditional institutions rose up to protect civilians against the deadly "messiahs"—the uneducated and undisciplined government troops on the one hand, and the unspeakably cruel and merciless RUF on the other. Paramount chiefs, men's secret societies, and the traditional hunter/ warrior societies faced off government soldiers, while others initiated ceremonies and performed rituals that would make an unarmed man "bullet-proof". Both educated and uneducated enrolled and were initiated into these rituals. Adherents went out into the bush, with nothing more than a loincloth and some charms, to confront bullets. These acts may be indicative of the level of their desperation, the strength of their traditional beliefs, or both.

When all these things had come to pass, Sierra Leoneans finally grasped that their problem went beyond the RUF. The provincial towns of Bo and Kenema virtually seceded from the state; setting up their own local militias and cooperating with foreign ECOMOG troops from Nigeria and Guinea to ensure their protection. This gave rise to the Civil Defence Forces (CDF), which later would play a significant role in supporting the regime of President Ahmad Tejan Kabbah, as well as an ambiguous role in the anarchy of the countryside. Sierra Leoneans began referring to those wreaking havoc on them as "sobels", or, "soldiers by day, rebels by night".[4] If the civil populace had come to this realization, the NPRC government was reluctant to make any public acknowledgement. Anyone familiar with cultures in which communication expresses significant meanings through parables and allegories would have recognized the invention of the term "sobels" as a clear message to the whole country that elements within the national army were engaging in rebel activities. Did the government of the day understand and act on this message? The Strasser NPRC tried to suppress the use of the term. The term persisted.[5]

The populace was no longer welcoming the young "messiahs" who had unleashed anarchy on them. Instead, the NPRC was told it had overstayed its welcome. Typically, the majority of people affected by the war find it difficult to remember that the NPRC may have made positive contributions to the country. The painful misery and shameful disgrace of living in displaced persons or refugee camps after losing everything have erased their memories. Most people have forgotten the irony that the RUF first came into being with the supposed intention of ending APC misrule and corruption; and that the NPRC overthrew the APC government because the latter was unwilling and unable to repel an already derailed RUF revolution.

Confronted with the inability of the NPRC to bring peace or provide coherent government, pressure was building to replace the soldiers with a civilian alternative. It must be remembered that the political classes in the provinces had been effectively excluded from governance since the introduction of the one-party state in 1978. Senior Interim National Electoral Commission officials insisted, against all odds, on holding elections in a climate of seeming anarchy. The international community jumped on this bandwagon and prescribed that the only way to get rid of what had become the unpopular and unacceptable NPRC government was by holding elections. The NPRC reluctantly agreed to elections. But before the promised elections could take place, a palace coup would see the replacement of Valentine Strasser by Brigadier Julius Maada Bio (in January 1996).

Maada Bio reportedly made contact with the RUF for a negotiated settlement to the war that had paralysed the country. Instead of seeking consensus and cooperation, the Sierra Leone nation polarized into two camps: pro "elections now" and pro "peace before elections". The country became absorbed in seminars, workshops and public relations rhetoric that focused not on the critical issues, but on exploiting public sentiment. For its part, the Maada Bio NPRC government wanted the elections postponed to build on the peace process that had been initiated. Opponents interpreted these attempts as a ploy to prolong its stay in power.

The civil populace was fed up with the NPRC government and its army. Nonetheless, there was need for an army, just as there was need to end the rebel menace. In this atmosphere of confrontational politics, one simple option was ignored: the formation of a government of national unity, consisting of all the active participants at that material moment, might have expedited an end to the wanton destruction of the country.

ELECTIONS AT ANY PRICE: BUT THE PRICE WAS MORE WAR

It was quite clear that elections and peace were not mutually exclusive choices for the country. It was also very obvious that a mechanism could and should have been found for harmonizing these two complementary choices. This should have been recognized, thoroughly analysed and evaluated, and a policy formulated to come into effect in 1996. Instead, divorce was introduced. The people were presented with a choice between peace and elections. The inherent assumption was that holding elections would bring peace back to the country. However, this hope was not fulfilled. An opportunity for peace was missed because a vocal minority refused to understand that an absolute military victory of one side over all the others in Sierra Leone's civil war was impossible, and thus the protagonists were obliged to cooperate.

Elections were held, although they were not country-wide. The first Kabbah government took office under difficult conditions. One year after the elections, the fallacy of the assumption that elections alone would bring peace became obvious. Despite the elections, the nation was still at war. The situation was getting even worse, with the war growing ever more savage. Elections alone, and by only a section of society, cannot form democracy.

The political classes and their professionals, who designed and canvassed the experiment in social engineering that was "elections now", deserve to be condemned for their conduct during this period of the country's history. Instead, it has taken them approximately four years to see themselves re-entrenched. In this period, they have perhaps developed enough confidence to go out of their way to bring the RUF and the SLA into town and into government. One day, perhaps they will explain to Sierra Leoneans that this achievement was worth the mutilation, death and destruction that has been inflicted on the nation since 1996. Otherwise, it is to be hoped that all concerned persons will find the moral courage to acknowledge their complicity or guilt, and ask the nation for forgiveness.

"We are fighting to uphold democracy." "The RUF wants to destroy the country." "The RUF wants to take over power by force at all costs." These are familiar enough defences for the government position. But it takes two to tango. Let us here state for posterity that in nine years of civil war, governments in Sierra Leone—including their professionals—and the RUF have committed unspeakable crimes against the nation and its people. Obviously, the charges against the RUF are easier to enumerate. In the making of their "revolution", the rebels engaged in inhuman atrocities against defenceless children, women and men who had nothing whatsoever to do with the government and the corruption the RUF claimed to be fighting. There has also been senseless destruction of national assets and private property. What is the RUF's defence in the face of the incontrovertible fact that during the course of its war, it has meted out inhuman treatment to persons who had nothing to do with government and governance? Children and even pregnant women have been abused and torn open. Limbs of people of all ages have been amputated, as well as whole communities burnt and properties destroyed or looted. Killing was indiscriminate; regardless of sex, age, creed or clan. Even RUF combatants have not escaped torture and summary execution. If the people had a choice, would they prefer misrule, corruption and neglect or naked brutalization and death at the hands of the RUF's self-proclaimed messiahs? Could any RUF leader sanely claim that these acts of barbarism against the people are in the defence of the same people? Does the RUF expect gratitude from these same people?

The charges against Sierra Leone's governments are no less grave. They pre-date the civil war. These charges derive from the fact that in a selfish quest for power and personal gain, the political class in Sierra Leone has failed to put the interests of the nation above its own. In this subjugation of national interests to personal and sectoral interests, the political establishment has violated the natural and human rights of the citizenry. The conduct of Sierra Leonean politicians created the necessary conditions for the birth of the RUF. The sufferings of the people before the start of the civil war, and at the hands of the RUF after the war started, were created and prolonged through the neglect of the nation's interests by the political classes, past and present. Yet, the people want peace.

· Were the efforts of governments in the war merely reactions to the actions of the RUF? If governments were not simply responding to RUF moves, why did the war drag on for so long, raging through successive governments?

It was not a surprise that, in such a chaotic political environment, on 24 May 1997 the government of President Kabbah was chased out of the country and Major Johnny Paul Koroma was sworn in as head of state under the Armed Forces Revolutionary Council (AFRC) junta. The AFRC was not officially recognized by any other country. International support remained with the civilian government-in-exile. Efforts to negotiate an end to this crisis became deadlocked, and in the end there was military confrontation.

The AFRC relied on elements within the national army (SLA) and rebel forces (RUF). The ousted civilian government relied on the regional ECOMOG forces led by Nigeria and the internally formed Civil Defence Forces. Finally, the AFRC was defeated and this resulted in the de facto disbandment of what remained of the army.

WHAT NEXT? OPTIONS FOR PEACE AND FEARS FOR THE FUTURE

Politics is about "goal attainment and control over one's environment".[6] Politics is a matter of power, and power in politics—power politics—is about the imposition of the will of one group of people in society on all the others. We consider "power" to be "the probability that one actor within a social relationship will be in a position to carry out his own will despite resistance, and regardless of the basis on which this probability rests".[7] In other words, "put simply and crudely, [power] is the ability to prevail in conflict and to overcome obstacles".[8] From the perspective of a civil war, the violent argument will last for as long as neither party is able to convince or coerce the other.

In the Sierra Leonean context, even though the protagonists have been reluctant to declare their absolute ambitions, power lies at the heart of their aims of war; power, and the financial rewards that go with it (in the case of Sierra Leone this means control of mineral resources). Almost ten years ago, when it first became public, the RUF claimed that its goal was to correct government misrule, official corruption, nepotism, public oppression and neglect of rural communities. Today, their claims ring hollow. Even when the opportunity arose under the AFRC (when the RUF was sharing power in Freetown), nothing was done that gives credence to these claims.

The NPRC overthrew the Momoh APC government with similar claims. Any good they may have done was overshadowed by the anarchy that prevailed during their rule. The old Freetown politicians have manoeuvred their way back into government using pretty much the same rhetoric. Sierra Leone's political debate is stale; and when it breeds violence that has become endemic, we may conclude that the political process has lost its way. It is an indication of the lack of responsible political leadership in the country that the various contenders have not evolved non-violent mechanisms for engaging in healthy competition or mutual accommodation in their pursuit of power. Alternative mechanisms for the acquisition and exercise of power should now be created.

For the time being in Sierra Leone, power politics seem to be "the way", despite the lip service paid to the ideals of the Lomé Accord. The ultimate desire of the actors still appears to be significantly influenced by hopes of ending the fighting with a quick military victory. It is only the non-availability of resources and feasible strategies that introduce delays.[9] The strategic situation seems blocked.

- The RUF remains a powerful obstacle for the government;
- the government is a powerful barrier for the RUF.

Each side is too weak to overcome the other; but each remains strong enough to continue fighting.

In this configuration of power (which is deadly for the people of Sierra Leone), one option for the protagonists is that they may agree to disagree: in which case the conflict may be rekindled at a later date.

The conflicting parties may also decide to be constructive and evolve a mutually acceptable compromise. However, for reasons of personal gain and greed, one party or elements thereof may believe one side enjoys some advantage over the other. In fact, neither side is able to force the other to accept unconditional surrender.

One can safely assert that most Sierra Leoneans have a strong desire to end the civil war in their country and establish a lasting peace. Even the fighting parties recognize this fact. They claim in the Lomé Accord that they are "moved by the imperative need to meet the desire of the people of Sierra Leone for a definitive settlement of the fratricidal war in their country and for genuine national unity and reconciliation".[10] The question then becomes, how to translate this desire for constructive peace into reality?

Three possible options for sustainable peace in Sierra Leone emerge:

Option 1: The RUF surrenders.
Option 2: The government surrenders.
Option 3: Both sides, genuinely committed to peace, cooperate in good faith.

In a civil war characterized by no possibility of a military solution, the third option has always been the most realistic. It is also the most constructive for sustainable peace in Sierra Leone. For that reason, it remains the best avenue for a promising future. This option should have been dispassionately identified, and thoroughly analysed and evaluated from the outbreak of the armed rebellion. As a result of the Lomé Accord, power-sharing became a reality: in October 1999 Foday Sankoh and Johnny Paul Koroma were appointed to chair key National Commissions (they became known popularly as "Vice-President for Minerals" and "Minister for Peace"), while certain of their lieutenants became ministers and deputy ministers in President Kabbah's government. The stand-off between the RUF and the old SLA should have ended; fighting with ECOMOG and UN forces should have been over. But the RUF did not disarm. At the moment when collaboration should have promoted confidence between the different parties, renewed violence led to the breakdown of trust and the arrest of Foday Sankoh.

Under what conditions is this imperative of cooperation in good faith possible? If peace is to be built through cooperative endeavours and compromise, who finally wins what and how? Who loses what and why? The Lomé Accord set the scene for finding answers to these questions, but the will to cooperate was missing. So where are the chief protagonists today, as we pursue the search for peace in the first year of the millennium?

THE REVOLUTIONARY UNITED FRONT: HAS THE PRODIGAL RETURNED?

The RUF was the child of bad governance in Sierra Leone. This offspring has shown itself capable of inflicting unimaginable, inhuman atrocities on the land and its peoples. Through the Lomé Accord the prodigal son has seemed ready to cooperate for peace, but it was always unclear whether RUF leaders were united and whether Sankoh had their loyal obedience. Will the RUF now accept that it cannot win power and hold it by military force? If weakness promotes negotiation, areas of strength could be abandoned in an effort for cooperation and peace.

THE GOVERNMENT: A NO-WIN SITUATION

For the government, it has been almost a no-win situation. Even in combat, the government has no "target". The populations behind rebel lines, including the rebels themselves, are Sierra Leoneans who should not be killed indiscriminately. They are the children and relations of Sierra Leoneans: the government cannot deliberately destroy them. While on the contrary, for rebels, everything material or human is a target. The politics of *terre brûlée*, which means megadeath and anarchy and chaos, is their war game. The government could never win the war; the RUF would never unilaterally surrender for peace. Thus, the same caution that had been applied in the prosecution of the war would be necessary for the government at any peace negotiation.

THE SIERRA LEONE ARMY: DISBANDED OR NOT DISBANDED?

The Sierra Leone Army is constitutionally sworn to protect the integrity of the nation. Events during the civil war in the country found it wanting in the discharge of its constitutional responsibilities. Its role in the overthrow of the elected government of President Kabbah and the failure of subsequent negotiations to resolve this crisis precipitated the need for armed intervention (external and internal) to dislodge the AFRC junta. A national army was defeated on its own soil, leading to the de facto disbandment of the SLA. SLA elements retreated into the bush, becoming the "rebels of the Okra Hills". President Kabbah's government acknowledged this fact. Subsequent political developments in the country, however, brought about a reversal of the official position. The official position today is that the army was never disbanded.

This political flip-flopping on the part of the government has adverse implications for future sustainable peace in the country. As should be expected, the army has not put forward any political agenda of its own. Yet there are stated and unstated demands that are worthy of note. By implication, no SLA member has been sacked as a result of the AFRC interregnum. This means, for a cash-strapped government, that all SLA members are owed back pay, plus benefits. The question of a downsized army becomes critical in the face of ongoing recruitment for a new army plus an old army that has never been disbanded. Even if some members of the old SLA choose voluntary redundancy or are made redundant, subject to prescribed criteria, redundancy pay would be an addition to the already outstanding back pay. These demands may be legitimate, but some SLA members may be culpable of criminal negligence and other crimes.

On a similar note, the Lomé Accord grants, inter alia, a blanket amnesty to all RUF members. This amnesty came fast on the heels of the fact that, soon after the reinstatement of the Kabbah government, a number of former SLA members were executed, having been found guilty of treason for their role in the AFRC coup. This begs the question of how many SLA living today, who may be reinstated into the new army, harbour grudges over these judicial killings? Are these the people who will serve in the new SLA?

What can we even hope for a "new army" that is being cobbled together? The British spent twenty years creating the excellent Defence Force of Independence: yet the authorities seem to think a few months of training will suffice for the army of the year 2000. These realities do not augur well for future reconciliation and sustainable peace in the country.

THE CIVIL DEFENCE FORCES: A SENSITIVE ISSUE

At their inception, the Civil Defence Forces (CDF) were created to protect the localities from RUF brutality. Within these theatres of operation, the CDF were under traditional moral sanctions. Everybody knew everyone else. Thus, even when they had guns, abuse of the power of the gun was unheard of while they operated within their locality. In a bid to contain the RUF, however, it became government policy to deploy these fighters outside of their normal domicile. Worse, this "recruitment and subsequent deployment" was not on the basis of any real contractual terms, or was on the basis of ill-defined conditions of service.

Give someone a gun among an unarmed population, with no contract and no logistical support, and the gun may turn in any direction. Undefined or ill-defined conditions of service are responsible for many of the excesses in Sierra Leone, and the Civil Defence Forces may not have been immune to these realities. Stories of their occult sacrifices and of the terror they are reported to have inflicted on civilians may merely have been temporarily stifled because of the domineering presence of regular and regulated but borrowed armies in their areas of operation. When peace is eventually negotiated or gained, by whatever means, and restrictions based on the current, undeclared state of emergency are lifted, these latent terrors may transform into renewed civil strife.

Absolute care needs to be taken in the management—and the disarmament—of the Civil Defence Forces. Many civil militiamen and women have been officially recruited in the government's quest to contain the RUF. A lot of the recruits are of school age. All they know of subsistence or survival is via the power of the gun. A large quantity of arms and ammunition has been distributed without a proper inventory. Worse still, their leadership may become interested in power politics. The CDF may not wish to be dumped at the end of the war without adequate compensation. The disarmament, demobilization and reintegration (DDR) process for RUF and SLA rebels is already inadequately planned and underfunded, and it does not even take into account the need to disarm and demobilize the CDF. These factors must be considered seriously by both government and donors if they wish to pursue lasting peace in the country.

Unemployed youth: a lost generation?

Unemployed, demobilized combatants would probably number in the thousands. They include those involved in militia organizations (this group could be referred to as "latent combatants"). These men (and some women) will increase the number of unemployed youths milling around the countryside or congregating outside Freetown's bars, wondering what the future will offer them ... wondering if they would not be better off returning to the gun-toting terror tactics of their war years.

We should ask whether the living standards of people on both sides of the conflict differ markedly? The latent combatants are as marginalized, displaced, starving and disillusioned, principally as a direct consequence of the war, as the armed rebels. All these young people are Sierra Leoneans and should benefit from the peace negotiations.

In the process of disarmament, demobilization and reintegration, the "R" is the part that has been neglected by government and donors alike. Large sums of money are available for UN-supervised camps, where armed fighters will bring in their weapons. But almost no resources have been allocated for technical training or retraining, for literacy and numeracy teaching, or for the establishment of ex-combatants in jobs. Nothing is planned for the psychological rehabilitation of ex-fighters whose youth has been spent in violence and brutality. Unless government and donors are willing to commit themselves politically and financially to the rehabilitation of this lost generation, there is little hope that the peace will be lasting or that Sierra Leone will regain its stability and prosperity. The government and any person or organization—including the RUF—who professes to fight for the interest of society should not negotiate at the expense of any Sierra Leonean.

BOUND TO COOPERATE: THE SHIFTING SANDS IN THE LOMÉ RIVER BED

The Lomé Peace Accord remains a bitter pill to swallow for many Sierra Leoneans. But "they love not poison that do poison need". The civil war in the country has ruined their lives, and Sierra Leoneans want to see an end to it. The doctors have prescribed a medicine that could cure the ailment. The government and insurgency groups have no alternative but to cooperate. This mutual need for cooperation is attributable, in part, to the failure of either side to defeat the other militarily. Both sides are also heavily dependent on external support for the pursuit of their true, undeclared ambitions. And as is normal in such cases, external support is always conditional.

By signing the Lomé Accord, the fighting parties—pushed by the African and international communities—have agreed to, and presented the people with, a peace plan. The guns have all but gone silent. This silencing of the guns is their gift to the people. The protagonists claim to be "moved by the imperative need to meet the desire of the people of Sierra Leone for a definitive settlement of the fratricidal war in their country and for genuine national unity and reconciliation". They claim to be "determined to foster mutual trust and confidence between themselves".[11] And while the events of early 2000—with RUF attacks north of Freetown, the kidnapping of UN soldiers and the capture and arrest of Foday Sankoh—give the lie to professions of "mutual trust" between the leaders, the Lomé Accord remains the document with which Sierra Leoneans must build "confidence between themselves".

The Lomé Accord offers the only opportunity to bring peace to this nation, which has been suffering for so long.[12] However, critical problems relating to justice, forgiveness, atonement and reconciliation remain. Here lie the shifting sands in the Lomé river bed: a careful reading of the Lomé agreement confirms that it is more about power and power-sharing than anything else. This is the theme throughout the document:

- "Transformation of the RUF/SL into a political party" (Article III);
- "Enabling members of the RUF/SL to hold public office" (Article IV);
- "Enabling the RUF/SL to join a broad-based government of national unity through cabinet appointment" (Article V);
- "The Commission for the Management of Strategic Resources ... whose chairmanship shall be offered to the Leader of the RUF/SL, Corporal Foday Sankoh" (Article VII);
- "The Government of Sierra Leone shall take appropriate legal steps to grant Corporal Foday Sankoh absolute and free pardon" (Article IX);
- "The Government of Sierra Leone shall also grant absolute and free pardon and reprieve to all combatants and collaborators" (Article IX);
- "The Government of Sierra Leone shall ensure that no official or judicial action is taken against any member of the RUF/SL, ex-AFRC, ex-SLA or CDF in respect of anything done by them" (Article IX).

Is the Lomé Accord about cooperation for peace, or complicity for power?

The Lomé Accord raises other important and related questions. Can there be peace without justice? Can there be reconciliation in the nation without any acknowledgement of guilt, and genuine atonement? Can there be social cohesion and harmony without equitable distribution of social, political and economic power in the nation? The issues inherent in these questions would appear to be the root causes of civil strife in Sierra Leone. This is the bitterness in the Lomé pill. To many Sierra Leoneans, it is a prescription for peace without justice. It is a prescription for superficial reconciliation without acknowledgement of guilt or genuine atonement. It is a prescription for false social cohesion in the midst of social, political and economic inequity.

At stake is not a quest for revenge for the sufferings inflicted on the people of that nation. No punishment can be sufficient to redress the inhumanity that has been inflicted. No Sierra Leonean whose father was killed, whose mother or sister was raped, or whose child was maimed can find solace or redress in judicial killing or imprisonment of the perpetrators of such crimes.

At stake is a genuine and concerted effort to redress the various forms of inequity inherent in the nation.[13] Then and only then can that nation know a sustainable silencing of the guns of civil strife. It would be a total abdication of responsibility if those culpable of criminal murder and maiming should come to expect gratitude from the relatives of their victims, never mind from their victims.

It would do the country as a whole, and particularly those who are culpable, no good to sweep the atrocities of the civil war years under the carpet in the name of reconciliation. The Truth and Reconciliation Commission could go a long way toward pre-empting and diffusing this kind of threat to sustainable peace.[14] If the TRC is successful, it may allow communities to receive back their children in a spirit of reconciliation. It would be unhealthy if the prodigal returns to exercise such influence on the parents, that the latter adopt the prodigal's evil ways, and violence returns.

Players of Sierra Leone's political game must learn to play it neat. They must cultivate the moral courage to recognize that any social system in which inequity is an integral part of its sociopolitical and economic foundation invites violence. When the central force becomes weak, social unrest becomes inevitable. Political stability requires cooperation against poverty and a joint commitment to respect the rules of the political game.

There is an urgent need for all aspirants to political leadership in the country to commit themselves to abide by the results of whatever is going to be the next leadership selection process. How and under what conditions the planned elections will be held is crucial. The politicians on show know they are bound to cooperate, whether they like it or not. That seems to be the only feature they have in common. But as regards the fundamental question: cooperation for what? There seems to be no constructive answer for the time being.

Notes

1   The Lomé Accord (or Peace Agreement) was signed on 7 July 1999 as an Agreement between the Government of Sierra Leone and the Revolutionary United Front of Sierra Leone.

2   On this issue, see Dennis J. D. Sandole, *Capturing the Complexity of Conflict*, London and New York: Pinter, 1999; T. Schelling, *Strategy of Conflict*, Cambridge: Harvard University Press, 1980.

3   Kabbah's tenure was interrupted by the regime of Major Johnny Paul Koroma (AFRC), May 1997–February 1998. The RUF shared power with Koroma's men during this period. As their partnership turned to rivalry, probably only the ECOMOG intervention that restored Kabbah to power avoided a showdown that might have seen the RUF oust the AFRC and seize power for itself.

4   See Jacky Cilliers and Peggy Mason (eds), *Peace, Profit or Plunder? The Privatisation of Security in War-Torn African Societies*, Halfway House: Institute for Security Studies, 1999; Bryan Posthumus, "Sierra Leone: Seeking a way out of the Abyss", in *Searching for Peace in Africa*, Utrecht: European Platform for Conflict Prevention and Transformation, 1999, pp. 372–382.

5   Today, after so much destruction—and after the phenomena coined in that one word marched into Freetown in 1997 and overthrew the civilian government of President Kabbah—the word and its singular meaning has become a part of the national psyche.

6   Karl W. Deutsch, "On the Concept of Political Power", *Journal of International Affairs,* Vol. XXI, pp. 332–341.

7   Max Weber, 1997, *The Theory of Social and Economic Organisation*, New York: Free Press, reprint edition, p. 152.

8   K. W. Deutsch, op. cit.

9   On this issue, see T. Schelling, op. cit.

10 Preamble of the Lomé Accord.

11 Ibid.

12 Chris Squire, *Agony in Sierra Leone*, Freetown: Ro-Marong Industries Ltd, 1996.

13 Chris Squire, *Ill-Fated Nation?* Freetown: Ro-Marong Industries Ltd, 1995.

14 At the very moment this manuscript is sent to the editor, we learn that the Sierra Leone Parliament has established a TRC.

CHAPTER 4

ARMS SMUGGLING, A CHALLENGING ISSUE FOR THE CUSTOMS SERVICE IN POST-WAR SIERRA LEONE

Nat J. O. Cole

ROLE OF THE CUSTOMS SERVICE IN A DEMOCRATIC STATE

The movement of goods and people across borders, both in peacetime and in times of war, is a feature common to every society. Various agencies are concerned with facilitation of this movement. However, the customs service is the government agency that plays the major role in the control and facilitation of the movement, not only of goods and people, but also vessels, aircraft and other modes of transport entering and leaving each country.

The customs service is thus charged with the responsibility of administering the laws regarding importation, exportation and transit of goods and the modes of transport of these goods. Such goods range from general, unregulated items to restricted goods like arms and ammunition, or medicines, to prohibited goods like illegal narcotics. The service is also responsible for the detection and prevention of smuggling. Accordingly, customs officers are engaged in coastal and border surveillance. Perhaps the most noticeable role of the customs service is that of revenue collection in the sphere of duties and taxes and assistance to industry in the form of tariff protection.

The service is therefore an agency dealing with the public in a variety of ways, from law enforcement to the protection of industry, the protection of the community and the collection of revenue. For our present purpose, however, the role of customs is confined to the enforcement of laws relating to the importation, exportation and transit of goods.

UNDERMINING OF CUSTOMS DURING THE WAR

In order to function effectively, customs generally operates through a central office in the capital, with other offices in strategic areas and, of course, outstations at points of entry and exit. The headquarters of customs in Sierra Leone are in Cline Town, Freetown.

Before the beginning of the civil war in 1991, the Sierra Leone customs service had a total of ten locations in the country. Apart from the headquarters, there were three posts in the Southern Province: one just by the Mano River Bridge, which links Sierra Leone and Liberia, the other two at Zimmi and Der-e-salam, towns bordering Liberia. There was one post at Kambia in the Northern Province. Two were in the Eastern Province: one at Beudu and the other at Koindu, both serving passengers and goods from Guinea and Liberia. At Freetown, the headquarters apart, there were customs representatives at the Parcel Post, at Sufferance Wharf, at Susan's Bay, and one post at Freetown's international airport at Lungi.

At the start of the war, customs, being a government agency, became a prime target of the rebels. "If you are a government employee you are an enemy." (A similar position was adopted during the conflict in Liberia.) The customs posts at Koindu, Beudu, Mano River Bridge and Der-e-salam were attacked and looted. Some officers were killed while others fled. The rebels then occupied these areas and used them as bases, bringing a complete breakdown of law and order to those areas. All types of goods, especially restricted and prohibited items like arms and ammunition and illicit drugs, found their way into the country through these rebel-held areas.

It should be pointed out that the Zimmi area is rich in diamond deposits, while the Koindu and Beudu areas are major agricultural areas, where coffee and cocoa are grown for export. The rebels controlled diamond mining, exporting both agricultural products and diamonds to Liberia in exchange for arms and ammunition and other items to fuel the war. Other difficult areas were controlled by Economic Community of West African States Monitoring Group (ECOMOG) forces, and government services were unable to monitor activities concerning production, distribution and commerce. Customs control in these areas was terminated, revenue dried up. This not only affected the budget, it also disrupted the exchange rate through the depletion of foreign exchange earnings. The role of customs in law enforcement, service to the community and revenue collection was thus extinguished in the affected areas.

IMPORTANCE OF CUSTOMS IN ARMS CONTROL AND ARMS REGULATION POLICY IN POST-WAR SIERRA LEONE

Sierra Leone does not manufacture arms, although there is one factory using one hundred per cent imported materials to produce shotgun cartridges. Thus, virtually all arms and ammunition, military weapons and shotguns are imported; they are therefore subject to restrictions on their importation. During a period of war, people often direct their ingenuity to the local production of weapons, especially guns. In the case of Sierra Leone this did not happen: arms control in the post-conflict era will therefore commence at the point of importation. The import restrictions imposed by law will be administered by the customs service.

The official importation of arms and ammunition is subject to a number of restrictions. There is first of all the condition that an importer of arms and ammunition must obtain a licence to import from the police before placing an order. Next there is the condition that owning and possessing a gun requires a licence from the police. This licence is renewable on a yearly basis, on payment of a fee. In the first two decades after independence, the regulation and licensing of weapons worked through local government institutions, and worked well. Centralization of the state, however, led people to neglect gun licensing laws altogether: party membership became more important than respect for the law.

In the current situation, where weapons abound in every village, peacemaking will depend partly on the success of Sierra Leone's government in registering weapons. Each weapon has a registration number. If it is carefully registered, its ownership and its travels can be traced. The exchange of computerized information between police and customs will become an important part of weapons control activity in post-war Sierra Leone. The installation of adequate computer equipment and appropriate training programmes should be an integral part of the reconstruction of customs services throughout the subregion, allowing for better international cooperation not only between neighbouring countries, but between West African countries and the International Criminal Police Organization (Interpol), and the International Customs Union.

It has been observed that whenever there are restrictions on the importation of a commodity, people tend to resort to smuggling by various means to get the commodity into the country. Since customs posts are situated at the gateway into Sierra Leone, with the role of enforcing importation and other laws for the safety of the community, the service has an important part to play in arms control. The procedures and the equipment for the physical examination of goods will have to be effective enough to meet the demands of the situation.

CHALLENGES FOR THE CUSTOMS SERVICE IN POST-WAR SIERRA LEONE

When peace and stability return to Sierra Leone, a lot of work will have to be done to repair the damage of the war. Burnt-out and looted buildings will have to be reconstructed, and capital will be required for the resumption of normal economic activity throughout the country. Thus, the public and the private sectors will require an extensive expenditure programme to bring things back to pre-war levels. The government will have to mobilize its tax system to try and collect as much revenue as possible to fund its numerous programmes. The private sector will want to recoup the losses it suffered as a result of the war, and in some cases may attempt to pay as little tax as possible and even to evade tax. One of the challenges the customs service will face will be to collect revenue in a situation in which there is reluctance to pay.

As has been mentioned, during the war smuggling increased considerably. Smugglers were interested in almost everything from farm produce and mineral resources flowing out of the country, to arms and illicit narcotics and various consumer goods coming into the country. It has been alleged that at the initial stages of the war, only the combatants were involved; but as the war progressed, business people jumped on the bandwagon and concentrated on the importation of consumer goods into the country without the payment of duty.

Various smuggling routes developed to bypass established customs posts, using forest paths through rebel-held territory. Smuggling by sea is easy to manage with a long coastline. Customs will therefore have to improve its surveillance network considerably when peace and stability return to the country. Border patrols will have to be intensified and more customs posts may have to be established along frequently used smuggling routes. Such measures will inevitably require additional staff and logistical resources, including motorbikes and communications equipment linking customs posts to their central controllers and to other security forces.

Another problem customs may have to handle concerns the attitude of smugglers if officials confront them in frontier areas. Notwithstanding the fact that the ex-combatants may have gone through a programme of rehabilitation, in the absence of gainful employment after the war, some may now take up smuggling, and in confrontational style. Thus, customs will have to be ready to face the challenge of armed conflict with smugglers. And we can expect these smugglers to be well armed with automatic weapons.

Illegal goods are smuggled into Sierra Leone across the borders by sea and land. The country has lengthy land borders with Guinea and Liberia and this has facilitated the smuggling of goods in general, and weapons in particular, across the borders of these countries. Refugees have been a dominant feature in the subregion in the past few years; up to 650,000 Sierra Leonean refugees are said to have been living in Guinea, where the Guinean authorities and population have extended the hand of friendship and hospitality to a remarkable degree. Their years of living "across two borders" will clearly influence both the smuggling and the security aspects of customs work.

It should be said, in passing, that the inherited colonial frontiers have little meaning for many border villagers, whose lands and families may lie either in Guinea or Sierra Leone; in Liberia or Guinea; in Liberia or Sierra Leone. Some people consider themselves equal citizens of two countries. The maintenance of peaceful frontiers will serve the interests of all three member states of the Mano River Union (Guinea, Liberia and Sierra Leone). Greater collaboration between their frontier security and customs forces would strengthen all three states at the expense of the smugglers and arms traders who undermine their mutual security.

There is a direct relationship between the trade, tariff and other policies existing in a country and the level of smuggling to and from that country. A low-tariff country in general may have little or no problem with the smuggling of goods into its boundaries. Again, if the laws regarding the importation of arms and ammunition and illicit drugs are significantly different among neighbouring countries, then it is clear that smuggling will exist.

Before the war the policy regarding the possession of arms and ammunition in Liberia was quite different from the restrictive policy existing in Sierra Leone. Accordingly, arms and ammunition were smuggled from Liberia to Sierra Leone, at a time when the people's only violent activity was hunting. Post-war control of arms and ammunition will depend in part on the arms policies existing in the countries within the MRU. Attempts must be made to harmonize trade, tariff, drug and arms and ammunition policies within these countries if the issue of smuggling, especially of arms and ammunition, is to be got under control.

CHAPTER 5

ARMS REGULATION, A CHALLENGING ISSUE FOR THE POLICE FORCE IN POST-WAR LAW AND ORDER ENFORCEMENT

J. P. Chris Charley

Sierra Leone became a crown colony in 1808, and by 31 August 1896 Britain had extended its authority to the whole area known as the provinces. To secure these areas, Britain set up a force known as the "Frontier Force", which later became the Sierra Leone Police Force (SLPF). The police force was patterned and developed on the lines of the British policing system. Initially, the force established and maintained standards of policing similar to those of other British colonies and was acclaimed as one of the best and most well-trained police forces in West Africa.

In 1961, the country gained independence. In 1964, the Police Act was passed in Parliament defining,

1. The functions of the police and the methods of its control.
2. The methods of appointment of police officers.
3. The powers and duties of police officers.
4. Service delivery strategy.
5. The disciplinary control of police officers.

INSTITUTIONAL UNDERMINING OF THE POLICE

The police force is one of the national institutions that has suffered most from the long process of state decay in Sierra Leone. Even before the introduction of the one-party constitution in 1978, due to political interference the outlook of the police gradually changed. From an institution that expected to serve the people, the police became politically compromised and perceived as existing to satisfy the objectives of politicians. Nothing illustrates the politicization of the police better than the changing status of its commander. The Inspector-General of Police was made a member of the ruling party, the All People's Congress (APC). He was later appointed a minister of state.

This acute politicization of the police force continued after 1985, when Siaka Stevens handed power to the head of the army, Major-General Joseph Momoh. As a result of the institutionalized politics of the promotion of political alliance to the detriment of professional ethics and efficiency, all facets of police work, including discipline, promotions, transfers and general operations, took a nosedive. The police officers on the ground lost not only self-esteem, but also the drive to perform, since their career was determined by who they knew, rather than their performance. To prove their commitment to the governing party and in the effort to get ahead in their career, some police officers had to indulge in either extra-legal or outright illegal activities. It is therefore no surprise that the public developed deep-seated grudges not only against the ruling party, but also against the police. This anti-government sentiment found expression not only in the lack of public confidence in the police as a neutral and non-partisan national law enforcement institution, but also an attitude of withholding all forms of cooperation from an organization that the general public saw as an instrument of oppression, coercion and corruption.

This negative perception of the police force found new expression in 1991. One of the Revolutionary United Front's (RUF) justifications for its declaration of war on the APC-led government was the accusation that the Sierra Leone Police Force was safeguarding only the selfish interests of the governing APC party, to the detriment of the collective national interest of the state and its citizens. The terrifying rebel war led to the near collapse of policing in Sierra Leone. The public saw the police force become more and more ineffective. This was compounded by the military regimes of Valentine Strasser, Julius Maada Bio and, later, Johnny Paul Koroma.

SIERRA LEONE POLICE FORCE IN DISTRESS

By 1996, when—as a result of popular pressure—the country held its first democratic multi-party elections for a generation, the police force was recognized as an institution in crisis. The force lacked the basic equipment to deliver its statutory services. Pens, paper, book registers were not available. Logistical support in terms of computers, photocopiers, vehicles and communication facilities was badly needed. In addition, most police buildings, including living quarters, had become uninhabitable through neglect, and were in a serious state of disrepair—if they had not actually been vandalized and destroyed.

This terrible situation was further aggravated on 6 January 1999, when a combined force of the Armed Forces Revolutionary Council (AFRC) and the RUF invaded Freetown and seized control of over half of the city, including State House. Following this attack, the Sierra Leone police experienced the worst atrocities the country has ever endured. More than two hundred police personnel and their dependants were killed in the most brutal circumstances. It is felt that the RUF was taking vengeance on the Sierra Leone police, which had been responsible, during the 1998 treason trials, for prosecuting members of the AFRC/RUF junta. Some of the accused had been found guilty and executed.

At the very moment when the country has need of competent and impartial police to help with the disarmament, demobilization and rehabilitation of former fighters during the implementation of the Lomé Peace Agreement, the national police force of Sierra Leone faces a Herculean task. We have already discussed the ways in which the police institution was undermined; the Police Advisory Council wrote in 1994:

> The image of the S.L.P [Sierra Leone Police] has deteriorated in recent times from the figure of a friend and social helper to a villain who is both ineffective and corrupt. This image has consequently adversely affected the relationship between the police and society. Poor people have been victims of the preoccupation of the police. This state of affairs has led to further loss of confidence by the public cooperation without which police work can hardly be successful.[1]

Therefore, one of the priority tasks facing the police in any genuine attempt to contribute to disarmament, arms control and arms regulation policies is reorienting the public psyche. The police must convince Sierra Leonean citizens that it is indeed a neutral player in the game of national politics. There is the need for a realistic programme of action to eradicate the public's deeply rooted distrust of and lack of confidence in their national police force.

In the effort to achieve the above and other objectives, including the optimum use of human and material resources, the police force is currently striving to process changes, reforms and comprehensive reconstruction. This important and very difficult work is going on with the determinant and highly appreciated expertise of the Commonwealth Police Development Task Force (CWPDTF) and the United Nations. In a recent article[2] the Acting Inspector-General of Police (head of the CWPDTF) wrote:

> For the past 15 years, police officers have rarely been provided with uniforms or basic equipment. The state of police barracks and stations throughout the country is truly appalling: many lack easy access to clean water; toilet facilities (where they exist) are primitive; and basic hygiene and disease control are almost non-existent. The cell accommodation in all police stations fails to meet international standards. This not only breaches the human rights of the prisoner, but also those of the arresting officer, who is obliged to detain suspects under inhumane conditions.

> Until the November 1999 budget, a constable was paid only Le 41,000 (US$15) per month. As a result, he/she would often supplement their income through corrupt practices, such as manning makeshift checkpoints. Wages have effectively been doubled, however, following the decision (in the budget) to replace the compensatory rice allowance with cash. Nevertheless, the salary barely meets daily requirements. A consequence of the SLP's neglect is that the general public has lost confidence in the efficiency and probity of the force.

LOCAL NEEDS POLICING

For its renaissance, in the interest of the nation and its citizens, and with the return to the country of a new commitment to forms of democratic governance, the Sierra Leone Police Force has opted for what it calls Local Needs Policing, or Community Policing.

Local Needs Policing is defined as "policing that meets the expectations and needs of the local community, and reflects national standards and objectives".[3] This means that the policing services provided by the Sierra Leone police must be tailor-made to the specific realities of situations prevailing in the community. This form of policing demands regular consultation with the community, so that the force can know what the people want from them. This recognizes that different communities have different needs, and that for policing services to be effective and worthwhile, they must acknowledge what ought to be achieved on the ground.

In this form of policing, local policing needs are delivered through a Local Command Unit, which is "a body of people, effectively and efficiently managed, accountable and with devolved authority, designed to deliver the policing needs of the local community".[4]

In the new Mission Statement (August 1998) of the Sierra Leone Police Force, the following declaration of faith gives a clear idea of what are, from now on, the strategy, ideals, values and priorities of the national police:

> We will respect human rights and the freedom of the individual; we will
> be honest, impartial, caring and free from corruption; we will respond to
> Local Needs; we will value our own people; we will involve all in
> developing our policing priorities.[5]

That is what Local Needs Policing is all about. Armed with these clearly spelled-out aims and objectives, the police intends, among other things, to win public confidence by offering reliable, efficient and accountable police services; the force is setting out to overcome the crisis of confidence that has characterized the police–population relationship.

The citizens would then understand that they and the police are in a partnership to enhance their security. They would understand that they too have a stake in the process. Within this new professional and ethical context, the job of maintaining law and order would cease to be perceived as the exclusive responsibility of the police, and would become one of the nation's commonly shared goals.

This new vision of the place and role of the police force in Sierra Leone justifies the stance on the obligation of the citizen, as contained in one of the policy documents:

> ... that an able bodied civilian cannot lawfully refuse to aid a constable
> whose own exertions are insufficient to effect an arrest, and that the
> citizen retains the right to protect his home and his family against
> criminal attack.[6]

Each citizen should participate in the preservation of his or her own security. The underlying assumption is that the police, and the community it serves, must reach consensus on the values that ensure the protection of life and property, in a joint effort to ensure a peaceful, stable and progressive society.

The most significant feature of this type of Local Needs Policing is that it does not alienate the community from the police, as has been the case for quite a long time now. This is because the community itself identifies its needs and what it wants from the police. Different communities have different security needs. In this context, the community can better identify itself with the operations of the police: this provides an ideal recipe for improved service delivery.

Pilot Local Needs Policing programmes have already been set up in Freetown (Congo Cross Police Station, Kissy Police Station), Waterloo Police Station and Bo Police Station. It is anticipated that the programme will eventually be extended to cover the whole country. The initial community response to these pilot projects has been quite encouraging. With appreciable injections of appropriate logistics and infrastructure, there is no doubt that such a strategy will help bridge the gap between the police force and the community. With personnel now being able to maintain contact with the community—courtesy of bicycles and motorcycles donated by the Commonwealth Police Development Task Force—mobility has been greatly enhanced. This new mobility alone has resulted in a remarkable reduction in public apathy (or outright hostility) toward the police.

This is why bicycles are preferable to motor vehicles. While the motor vehicle separates the police officer from the population, a bicycle brings them closer together. In terms of speed and mobility too, the bicycle is well adapted to the terrain of bush paths and city alleyways, although there is an obvious role for motor vehicles as support vehicles, both in terms of their speed across flat surfaces, and because they can transport several officers together as a team.

The concept of Local Needs Policing has also helped us decentralize our operations. This is a great advantage. Before, all major decisions by the police were taken in Freetown at the national Police Headquarters. This has changed. The decision-making process has been decentralized, in recognition of the fact that if the police is to serve the community well, it must be willing and able to react speedily to issues as they arise. In pursuit of this objective, the police force has appointed Regional Commissioners in three of the four regions of the country, that is, the East, South and North. These Commissioners are directly responsible for the day-to-day operations of the regional command. They can take and implement decisions without referring in advance to Headquarters in Freetown (in Western Area).

With this arrangement in place, the police can now swiftly and adequately respond to situations in their own regions, and thus put an end to the allegations that the Sierra Leone police operates on some "fire brigade" mentality, moving from one crisis to another across the country without building security in the community.

DISARMAMENT, THE POLICE AND CIVIL SOCIETY

It is clear that Local Needs Policing is based on a new concept of partnership between police and people. The rest of this article will examine the way in which such a concept of partnership can benefit the process of disarmament, demobilization and reintegration (DDR), the success of which is essential for law and order to reign again in Sierra Leone. We shall start by considering the framework of firearms rules and regulations within which the police will be working.

One area where the community and civil society can contribute effectively to assist the police is law and order enforcement in the context of arms regulation. Civil society must contribute to the much-needed national debate concerning the enactment of gun and arms control legislation. In a budding democracy, civil society has an important role to play in prevailing upon its elected representatives to pass laws pertaining to the manufacture, importation, storage and possession of firearms, especially the small arms and light weapons that are most commonly used to make war in the subregion.

The Economic Community of West African States (ECOWAS), at its twenty first ordinary session of the Authority of Heads of State and Government in Abuja, Nigeria on 30–31 October 1998, adopted a Declaration of a Moratorium on the Importation, Exportation and Manufacture of Small Arms and Light Weapons in West Africa. This positive step must be replicated by national legislatures, including the Sierra Leone Parliament. For this to be a reality, the support of civil society is necessary, since the organizations of civil society are, apart from their elected legislators, the only obvious voice of the people in national and international debate.

Recognizing that the unregulated circulation of weapons is a threat to civil order, the police force has a primary interest in the success of the DDR process. In facing the challenge of building an arms-free Sierra Leone, the police force intends to carry out a purpose-directed sensitization exercise to change the attitude of the citizens, and to mobilize civil society in support of police objectives. It is necessary that the community appreciates the importance of disarmament and the vital necessity of arms regulation. Citizens must be made to realize that effective disarmament is a prerequisite for the community's security and lasting development. They need to recognize that no meaningful socio-economic development can take place without their contribution to the process of peace, security and confidence-building through disarmament and arms control. Such a contribution can only be realistic and appreciable when every citizen fully knows and is genuinely aware of his or her important, and determinant, role.

Although each parent and each citizen should recognize his or her personal responsibility in the matter of public order, we need to mobilize the citizens in a concerted campaign. It is for this reason that the police force must seek partnership with civil society. If civil society means "citizens organized around a common interest and objective", then the common objective that we are offering is "peace through disarmament".

It is expected that with the new police structures and mechanisms in place, civil society can play an essential role in ensuring that the country becomes arms-free and violence-free. After all, most of the people who carried the arms in the first place are part of the wider community. They too must realize that their decision to lay down their weapons and take part in the peace process would be a good thing, not only for the nation as a community, but also for themselves as individuals. This requires careful confidence-building: the former fighters must be convinced that when they give up their arms and enrol in the disarmament, demobilization and reintegration programme, their personal security will not be jeopardized.

We must never forget that these gun-toting men and women, these ex-combatants, are our own people. They are our brothers and sisters. A cooperative civil society can achieve much through dialogue with them; making them understand that they are killing and maiming their own people. No other group of people, not even the United Nations with all its expertise and goodwill, can do this better than the leaders of our own society.

Without the support of the population, how can the police expect to collect the secret illegal arms that lie buried across Sierra Leone? A positive leadership role by civil society would definitely speed up the disarmament process. Only the local leaders of civil society in the communities can identify areas suspected to contain hidden arms and ammunition, thanks to their knowledge of the environment and their kinship with the ex-combatants. As the Inspector-General wrote at the start of 2000:

> A great deal has already been achieved, but there is still much to be done to create a strong Police Force. A tremendous amount of sensible policing—backed by civil society—still needs to occur. Unless an environment conducive to holding free and fair elections is created over the course of the next year, Sierra Leoneans will be unable to exercise their right to vote in peace and without intimidation.[7]

Civil society is indeed an integral player in the disarmament and arms regulation process, and in producing a lasting peace. Collaborative efforts with the new police force would strengthen both civil society and Sierra Leone's peace.

WHAT TO DO?

Having recognized the police force as one of the key players in an arms-free Sierra Leone, the key question remains: can the police force in its present state effectively and efficiently participate in law and order enforcement in post-war Sierra Leone?

The answer to this question, even to the casual observer, is "No". As seen earlier, during nearly a decade of brutal and bloody civil war, nearly all police installations and equipment have been destroyed. Over the years, the force has suffered victimization, neglect and deprivation, which has not only sapped the self-confidence of the personnel, but has further eroded public trust in the force. Since the period of Siaka Stevens, the police force has been transformed from an organization whose members drew respect and admiration from law-abiding citizens, and fear from would-be offenders, to one that draws only scorn and outright contempt from the public.

Moreover, as a result of the war, military and paramilitary forces have taken over nearly all the statutory responsibilities of the police, leaving the police as a passive observer. Lacking even the basic logistics necessary for policing, the Sierra Leone Police Force has found itself trapped between a rock and a hard place. The intent to assume primacy in villages, towns and city streets is constrained by the absence of logistics and equipment. The unavailability of these essentials has forced the military and paramilitary forces to continue performing statutory police functions that they would undoubtedly prefer to give up, but for the security vacuum that this may provoke.

In order for the police to provide adequate services for ensuring an arms-free Sierra Leone, and to bring impartial enforcement of law and order throughout the country, the national police force must, in the short run, be assisted in the following areas:

- **Communications**
    - solar-powered or battery-operated VHF and HP hand-held sets; detective tape recorders and cassettes;
    - video recorders;
    - computers, word processors, typewriters, projectors; and
    - photocopiers, office cabinets and other office supplies.

- **Back-up intervention**
    - customized meshed trucks/pick-up vans fitted with communications technology;
    - bicycles;
    - motorcycles;
    - four wheel-drive patrol cars for bush patrols;
    - small cars for city patrols;
    - specialized vehicles like personnel carriers, patrol cars, tow trucks, cesspit trucks, fuel and water tankers;
    - spare parts (tyres, tubes, etc.);

- tear gas canisters, riot shields, helmets and masks, smoke guns and smoke cans, rubber bullet guns and rubber bullets, handcuffs;
- metal and weapon detectors, bombs/explosive detectors;
- landmine detectors;
- megaphones; and
- uniforms and other accoutrements, e.g. raincoats and rain boots.

There are also serious infrastructure requirements for police stations and living accommodation, after years of neglect and destruction. A lot has been accomplished with Commonwealth and British support: health facilities, sanitation and water supplies to barracks have been improved as a first priority. But when one remembers the historical perspective, and the days when the Sierra Leone Police Training School existed with a proud tradition, producing many hundreds of competent police graduates for countries across the subregion, it is sad to see the wrecked buildings, the signs of fire and decay.

CONCLUSION

In concluding, we can only add that the list of assistance sought is in no way exhaustive. In the 1999 publication *The Sierra Leone Police: A Force in Distress*, a detailed needs assessment is fully discussed. In the recent past, and with the minimum of logistics, the SLPF has scored major successes, especially in the areas of armed robbery and smuggling—predicted aftershocks of the war. If the Sierra Leone police are provided with logistics and equipment, they will create an enabling environment for all personnel to enhance performance and deliver quality services to the community. This will be critical in restoring the confidence and respect of the people served.

Notes

[1] Sierra Leone Police, "Advisory Council Notes", No. 12, Freetown, 9 May 1994.

2   Keith Biddle, "Acting Inspector General of the Sierra Leone Police", *Bulletin of the Conflict, Security and Development Group*, London: King's College, London, Issue Number 5, March–April 2000, pp. 1–4.

3   Sierra Leone Police, *The Sierra Leone Police Force in Distress*, Freetown, 1999, p. 20.

4   Ibid.

5   Sierra Leone Police Force, *The Sierra Leone Police Force: Government Policing Charter*.

6   Sierra Leone Police Force's Policy Document: "Historical Development of the Police", p. 2.

7   Keith Biddle, op. cit., p. 4.

CHAPTER 6

ARMS CONTROL POLICY UNDER THREAT: DEALING WITH THE PLAGUE OF CORRUPTION

Abdulai Bayraytay

INSTITUTIONALIZING CORRUPTION

Sierra Leone is a country blessed with abundant resources, especially diamonds. This wealth would have turned Sierra Leone into an earthly paradise but for corruption and mismanagement.

The bulk of Sierra Leone's wealth is derived from the sale of diamonds. The first diamond mines were discovered in the 1930s. Unfortunately, the political leadership, since independence in 1961, became very much entrenched in the diamond trade and its attendant trail of massive corruption. For instance, Siaka Stevens, soon after he was made Prime Minister in 1968, quickly turned diamonds into a political issue. The policy of official diamond smuggling is illustrated by the fact that officially recorded diamond exports plummeted from over 2,000,000 carats in 1970 to 95,000 carats in 1980, and then just 48,000 in 1988.[1]

State diamond mining was the first of the state institutions to be corrupted. Perhaps the fundamental consequence of corruption was to divide the society into two distinct categories of citizens.

- The haves: the blessed few in power.
- The have-nothings: the great majority of the population.

The first class of citizens became hugely rich thanks to the predatory politics of national wealth smuggling; and the second class sank deep into the abyss of misery.

It is consequently not a surprise that the United Nations Development Programme's Human Development Index ranks Sierra Leone as the least developed country in the world: life expectancy at birth is pegged at 33.6 years; the adult literacy rate is 30.3 per cent (1999).[2] The main responsibility for this distressing situation lies with persistent political mismanagement and its most disturbing consequence, corruption.

Since Sierra Leone gained independence in 1961, governments have never really been accountable to the people. Transparency and accountability are unknown to the vocabulary of the country's political establishment. Financial mismanagement was compounded by the systematic destruction of the most important institutions of the state. During the reign of one-party politics—lasting almost three decades—institutions like the judiciary, the Accountant and Auditor General's departments, the police and the army became politicized. Since independence, governmental administrations and ministries have found it very difficult to produce balance sheets as a way of accounting for budgetary resources allocated. This situation cannot be divorced from the overcentralization of the powers and operations of government, which succeeded in breeding corruption at almost all levels in Sierra Leonean society.

What is corruption? Many authors have tried to answer this question.[3] Empirical investigations show that corruption is a multifaceted phenomenon with economic, political as well as cultural roots.[4] For the sake of this analysis, corruption is considered to be "the misuse of public power for private profit": in other words, corruption involves behaviour on the part of officials in the public sector, whether politicians or public servants, in which they unlawfully enrich themselves (or those close to them) by the misuse of the public trust bestowed upon them.[5]

THE GREAT ILLUSION OF THE NPRC INTERREGNUM

On 29 April 1992, young Sierra Leonean military officers staged a *coup d'état* that ousted the All People's Congress (APC) regime. The military cited corruption, mismanagement and the rebel war as the principal catalysts for the coup. A National Provisional Ruling Council (NPRC) was formed. Captain Valentine Strasser, chair of the NPRC, declared that Sierra Leone had been for nearly three decades in the iron grip of "an oppressive, corrupt, exploitative, and tribalistic bunch of crooks under the APC Government". Concluded Valentine Strasser: "Our schools and roads are in a terrible state as a result of mismanagement."[6]

NPRC members were initially hailed as the messiahs of Sierra Leone by a population worn down by corruption, poverty and war. Within a year, however, the NPRC members had become entangled in corrupt practices. An editorial in *New Breed*, captioned "Villains or Redeemers", implicated NPRC chairman and head of state Captain Strasser in a US$ 4.3 million diamond deal at the Antwerp market.[7] This state of affairs, combined with issues of human rights violations, persuaded civil society to demonstrate a new unwillingness to cooperate with a junta that had damned its predecessor for political ineptitude. Their stance was clearly vindicated by the incredible revelations of massive corruption in the respective commissions of inquiry set up by the NPRC.[8]

It is against this distressing state of military rule that the Revolutionary United Front (RUF) intensified its rebel terrorist campaign against the government (and the people) of Sierra Leone. The RUF had inaugurated its military revolt on 23 March 1991 against Siaka Stevens's successor at the head of the APC one-party state, Joseph Momoh. Its leader, retired corporal Foday Sankoh, had ranted that the APC government should introduce political reforms as a basis for addressing the country's mismanagement and corruption.[9] The NPRC had promised to end the RUF revolt: but the ensuing military campaign brought only bloodshed and led the RUF to excesses of massive and indiscriminate violence.

WAR AND SMALL ARMS PROLIFERATION

According to the 1955 Ordinance on the import and export of arms and ammunition, "any person who imports into Sierra Leone any small arm or small arms and ammunition except under an import licence ... shall be guilty of an offence".[10] Under the same Ordinance, "any person who possesses any small arm ... unless he is a holder of a current licence ... shall be guilty of an offence".[11]

These provisions were fairly applied during the 1960s and 1970s, when Sierra Leone's gun control laws provided a model for decentralized arms management and licensing. However, the one-party state did away with decentralized local government and gun control largely disappeared at the same time. The 1978 one-party constitution of Sierra Leone was silent over the availability, possession and use of arms. This led to the proliferation of handguns and the overt use of arms by some foreign business tycoons.

The regular military and paramilitary forces found themselves faced with parallel, privately owned, forces. During this period, a lot of arms trafficking took place, sometimes with the connivance of well-placed officers within the state's security apparatus.[12] In response to the 1978 constitution, section 166 of the 1991 constitution specifically prohibited the raising of private armies.[13] The advent of civil war brought massive proliferation of small arms and light weapons to Sierra Leone: but the war only exacerbated a situation of small arms proliferation that had already got out of hand.

The long and hard years of one-party rule in Sierra Leone were also characterized by political manipulation. The illegal accumulation of arms helped the country's politics to degenerate into violence: guns were used to intimidate voters into accepting candidates who were not of their choice. These methods undermined principles of good governance. The Central Organizing Committee of the APC, which selected candidates to represent the party in Parliament, undermined popular participation. Thuggery was introduced into the body politic of the state. Rich and influential politicians whose mandate was at stake flooded the political scene with arms, recruited unemployed youths as thugs, and encouraged them to unleash violence during election time.[14]

A classic example was the Ndorgborwusui crisis in Pujehun in the Southern Province during the 1982 general elections. Attempts were made to impose one Demby. He did not hail from Pujehun, but he was a blue-eyed boy of APC Vice-President Francis Mischek Minah, who came from that district. The electorate expressed its disgust by resorting to the use of arms in resisting APC tactics of political imposition. Pujehun is much closer to Liberia than Freetown, and this violent incident in Ndorgborwusui would have a direct link to the outbreak of the RUF rebel war in 1991. After the Ndorgborwusui crisis, many youths escaped to neighbouring Liberia, especially after thugs hired by the APC government brutally killed teacher Mustapha Kemokai.[15] The savage murder of Paramount Chief Momoh Kpaka immediately followed this;[16] it was perpetrated by APC thugs under the cover of the Special Security Division (SSD) paramilitary force. The notoriety of the SSD earned it the title of "Siaka Stevens's Dogs".

As political violence grew, so did the dissemination of firearms. Equally dangerous was its effect on the psychology of the Sierra Leone people. Violence during elections attracted strong condemnation, but it frightened most people into silence. Voters were scared off the political scene because of bloodshed, despite the fact that they are the ultimate holders of political sovereignty in a democracy.[17]

NO ONE IS INNOCENT

From the above it is clear that corruption in Sierra Leone transcended the phenomenon of just pilfering public funds: it was a struggle for state power. Stevens publicly opined in Krio that "usai yu tai kaw, na dae i dae eat"("a cow grazes where it is tethered"), thereby officially sanctioning corruption. It became a serious breach for a cabinet minister, for instance, to leave office without a fleet of houses and vehicles and a fat bank account. Corruption was the order of the day in Sierra Leone's government. More frightening, the whole nation seemed, in the end, to perceive the overwhelming evil as "normal". Popular thought came to accept that a successful politician was a rich politician. Hence, in spite of the exuberant national welcome accorded to the young military officers' government (NPRC) by the population (and even by certain leaders of civil society), corruption continued, unchecked.

Meanwhile, the war raged on. So did the NPRC's profusion of promises to eradicate corruption "in all spheres of public life" and to bring the war to a "speedy conclusion". None of their promises brought relief. The situation was desperate. It was in that desperation that the NPRC teamed up with the financier and mineral magnate Jean-Raymond Boulle.[18] To give the impression of ending the war, they decided to hire mercenary companies (they would prefer the title "security companies"). First came the Gurkha Security Group, through the British arms manufacturer J. and S. Franklin.[19] Later on, the South African-based Executive Outcomes was also contracted to put the rebels of the RUF at bay: Executive Outcomes' payment was arranged by assigning them to the lucrative diamond mining areas. These multinational security outfits not only spur Africa's conflicts for personal gain, they also become very interested in "protecting" the rich mining and diamondiferous areas of the country, in what has generally come to be considered as "security for diamonds".[20]

As war continued amid massive corruption, diamonds became the overriding factor in fostering arms availability. The illegal trafficking of diamonds is hugely lucrative. It attracted rogue or neighbouring states like

Liberia and Côte d'Ivoire, which flooded Sierra Leone with stockpiles of arms and ammunition in return for diamonds.[21] Other states served as transit points (Burkina Faso, Gambia, Togo). This trend of war combined with lucrative diamond trafficking attracted multinational corporations to "encourage" the RUF to control diamond-rich areas like Kono, Kailahun and Tongo fields, to name but a few, in exchange for arms.[22]

No one is innocent. This illicit mining was fostered by the beleaguered NPRC regime, which by all indications lacked the necessary power to check the flow of arms. The responsibility must be shared by Western diamond companies, including de Beers of South Africa and the Central Buying Organization in London, the Israeli, Hong Kong and Thai markets, and the Dutch and Belgian diamond markets, all of which have been cited in recent reports by the United Nations and international civil society organizations. Only in the year 2000 have serious moves been initiated by Western governments to curb the corruption in which their citizens and corporations have colluded so actively. Since 1995 (and thanks to the corrupt complicity of Western economic interests) Sierra Leone, with the presence of diamonds and their exchange for arms, has competed with Angola for the dubious honour of being the world's leading mercenary bazaar.[23]

Even as the present text was being finalized, the United Nations Security Council voted, on 5 July 2000, a total embargo on the sale of uncut diamonds from Sierra Leone (in response to a United Kingdom initiative that shows a welcome, if belated, commitment to what its Foreign Secretary has described as an "ethical foreign policy"). This boycott can only be effective if UN Member States take action to insist that their nationals, and the companies registered or active in their territories, refuse all purchases of uncertified diamonds passing through Liberia or arriving in Europe in the pockets of travellers. If the embargo is successful, it will cut the purchasing power of the RUF and other rebel groups.

Interestingly, while the government made underground purchases of fighting equipment, including AK47s, M16s and German-made bazookas, the RUF claim never to have imported any weapons into Sierra Leone. Rather, it claims to have accumulated its weaponry from "enemy forces". There are indeed many instances cited by the population of Sierra Leone of army officers selling weapons or ammunition to the RUF. To this environment of arms proliferation, the beleaguered government encouraged the addition of Civil Defence Forces (CDF), groups based on community hunters' associations. This gave rise to militia units like the Kamajors, Gbethis, Donsos and Tamaborohs in the name of self-defence.

Nine years of anarchy and chaos have led to the massive accumulation of weapons. The main victims have been innocent women and children. The dire consequences of the great proliferation of small arms and light weapons were blatant during the 25 May 1997 coup by the AFRC/RUF alliance, and later in the disastrous invasion of Freetown by the rebels in January 1999, with the loss of scores of lives and widespread human rights violations.

Overarching these problems is a state that is incompetent in handling economic, sociocultural and even political matters. The private sector, led mainly by transnational companies and organizations, has established its hegemony over all aspects of human endeavour, leaving only "nominal State security in the hands of governments".[24] Coupled with the squeeze on the finances of the Sierra Leonean economy through donor-imposed programmes, this has succeeded in producing an army that is much under-resourced. Thus the apparent collusion of the soldiers and rebels in arms trafficking, which later created in Sierra Leone's vocabulary the word that best summarizes the corruption of the state's security apparatus: "sobels", meaning "soldiers" by day and "rebels" at night.[25]

THE NEW START HAS NOT YET BEGUN

The elected government of President Ahmad Tejan Kabbah inherited a mountain of security-related challenges. Among these was legitimacy: "democratically elected" implies universal suffrage, when in fact the election was mainly limited to Freetown and the western end of the country. The plague of corruption was certainly another of Kabbah's government's toughest challenges. Handicapped by the AFRC's constant reminders of its limited electoral mandate and its limited control of security, the government seems unable to curb corruption. This is particularly unfortunate since corruption was advanced by the RUF as one of the major reasons for its rebel war.

Inasmuch as the scourge of corruption is concerned, nothing—or very little—has changed in Sierra Leone today. Corruption remains a cause and a consequence of bad governance and the collapse of the Sierra Leonean state. This is seen in the siphoning of funds from a parastatal like LOTTO, the national lottery. According to one newspaper, "British auditors discovered that the Sierra Leone government lost billions of leones over a period of two years which made LOTTO boss, Syl Harding, the highest "paid" parastatal manager in the country".[26] The lottery had annual sales running at about US$ 5 million. There are many examples of the government's failure to curb corruption. Two revenue collectors at the Customs Department were implicated in a Le 46 million racket at the Kambia Customs Post.[27] Within weeks, a *Standard Times* article implicated the Managing Director of the Sierra Leone Postal Services (Salpost) and his management team in the misappropriation of Le 154 million between 1 July 1994 and 31 December 1995.[28]

Just a few months after the democratically elected government was reinstated by the Economic Community of West African States Monitoring Group (ECOMOG) in March 1998, the government unearthed a Le 800 million loss (equivalent to US$ 470,000) in the Ministry of Finance. Finance Minister James Jonah later attributed this to corrupt civil servants.[29] In August of 1998, billions of leones were squandered on the repair of government quarters allocated to ministers.[30] This was followed by another scandal on 17 January 1999, when the sum of Le 1.2 billion, meant for teachers' salaries, was allegedly stolen in the ministry, with the rude connivance of senior police officers.[31] In August 1999, the erstwhile Minister of Agriculture and his Director-General were accused of embezzling US$ 1.5 million of World Bank resources. Unusually, both were arrested and detained and are now facing criminal charges.[32]

Almost none of these scandals have led to arrest and prosecution. A culture of impunity reigns, aided by acts of criminal arson, which also go unpunished. As a result of corruption allegations, perpetrators have more than once resorted to the burning down of offices. A probe into the management of the national lottery eventually led to the burning of the office. This was followed by the burning down of the government medical stores on 12 September 1999.[33] The irony is that we actually seem to be institutionalizing a new "pyromaniac culture" in Sierra Leone. The rebels burn down public offices, and so do the holders of public office or civil servants, as demonstrated by the burning of the Central Bank and the Treasury in the wake of the AFRC coup of 25 May 1997.

A parliamentary inquiry has revealed massive corruption at the Sierra Leone Telecommunications Company (Sierratel). The government rejected the report on the basis that a wrong procedure was used in the inquiry.[34] The Electricity Company has been rocked by repeated corrupt scandals over the years, but a commission of inquiry has yet to produce a report. Government ministers have been said to be involved in corrupt deals in many instances. A case in point is the implication of the Presidential Affairs Minister in a US$ 200,000 mining concessions deal; and then in another US$ 3.5 million arms deal at the height of the rebel invasion of January 1999.[35]

The allegations of corruption attained a new significance when the nation was shocked by the allegation that the Chief Justice, Desmond Luke, had squandered grants awarded by the United States Embassy for the renovation of the Law Courts and their equipment with a generator and modern law books.[36] That such allegations should touch the judicial arm of the state, normally a key component in the fight against corruption, is unfortunate, to say the very least. The judicial system should not only be independent of the government, it should also provide a model of integrity.

In the fight for good government, the Sierra Leone Police Force and the Customs and Excise Department, key governmental institutions for any anti-corruption policy, are found wanting. Apart from the fact that Sierra Leone's political borders are porous, there are instances in which serving personnel from the security or customs services, charged with the responsibility of discouraging the supply of arms, sometimes connived with unscrupulous businessmen in illicit diamond and arms and ammunition trafficking.[37] What seems to have compounded this distressing trend are the poor salaries and appalling conditions of service within the forces. Years of bad political leadership have left these forces underequipped and undermotivated. According to one senior customs official (who spoke to us on condition of anonymity): "Officers at our unit are very much trained and qualified. The problem is not so much of the meagre salaries, but the lack of logistics for effective border operations."

The people were full of hope when the government of President Ahmad Tejan Kabbah was elected in 1997, even though only one part of the electorate was able to vote. This was meant to be the new start: a new civilian government with new, clean leaders was replacing the young military officers who had proved to be corrupt and incompetent. This government was again installed a second time—by ECOMOG—in March 1998, to clean up a new military mess. But the new face of President Kabbah did not provide new policies or a new style of clean government. Behind Kabbah, either in the wings or on the political stage, are too many old faces from old, discredited regimes.

PEOPLE AGAINST CORRUPTION: CIVIL SOCIETY ACTION

As a result of the government's inability to take significant action against the scourge of corruption, civil society groups in the country launched an anti-corruption campaign. Every opportunity was used to get the message to the president that corruption was a determinant security-related issue that must addressed most urgently.[38] This campaign attracted coverage in both the electronic and the print media.[39] Religious leaders from both churches and mosques joined the campaign, which culminated in meetings with President Kabbah and the holding of a national conference.[40]

The government responded, eventually, by setting up an Anti-Corruption Bureau.[41] The Bureau was created at a time when reports of the many government commissions of inquiry on corruption matters had not yet been produced. While the Bureau seems to rekindle hopes that there may be light at the end of the tunnel, its establishment was preceded by a heated debate in Parliament as Members of Parliament questioned the president's exclusive right to appoint its head.[42] A first sign for concern regarding the Bureau was when President Kabbah's nominee for the post of commissioner, Dr William Conton, rejected the offer after Parliament tried to probe into his 10-year income tax clearance for a house he was said to have rented out for Le 20 million per annum.

Notwithstanding this embarrassment, the establishment of the Anti-Corruption Bureau has been widely welcomed in Sierra Leone. The Bureau, if efficient in its functioning, can become a great instrument for good governance and peace in Sierra Leone. Let us examine the mission, the composition and the powers of the Bureau as enacted by Parliament.

According to the Anti-Corruption Act, the mission of the Bureau includes, among other issues:

- "The implementation of a national anti-corruption strategy and to investigate instances of alleged or suspected corruption referred to it by any person or authority or which has come to its attention, whether by complaint or otherwise and to take such steps as may be necessary for the eradicating or suppression of corrupt practices."
- The establishment of preventive mechanisms and education initiatives or campaigns intended to change the perception held by the nation about corruption. Actually, "the emphasis in the bill is on civic education, popular participation and cooperation ... rather than on the enforcement of the law against corruption".

The Bureau shall be headed by a commissioner, who shall be assisted by a deputy commissioner and auxiliary staff whose membership shall take into consideration the regional dimension of the country. The power of the Bureau is assured by its autonomy and independence; it shall be funded directly by Parliament and will therefore be directly answerable to it.

As such, it appears that the powers of the Bureau are extensive. They include: "to examine the practices and procedures of government ministries, departments and other public bodies, and to also determine whether a public official maintains a standard of living as that which is commensurate with his or her present or past official income, and also prosecuting anyone with public authority who misappropriates any donation in the benefit of the people of Sierra Leone."

However, it should be pointed out that the Anti-Corruption Bureau faces additional challenges, beyond its mission. One problem is the apparent conflict of interest with the functions and duties of the office of the Ombudsman as stipulated in chapter 8, section 146 of the 1991 Constitution of Sierra Leone (but yet to be established). Moreover, the principal complementary institution of the Bureau is the judiciary, which, at the moment, is not only understaffed and unable to effect speedy corruption trials, but has logistical problems as well. Without the support of an effective and efficient judicial process, the fight against corruption is condemned to failure.

Sierra Leone's situation cannot be considered in isolation, especially when the fight against corruption is related to the fight against the proliferation of small arms and light weapons. Sierra Leone's efforts need to be strengthened by similar initiatives and policies in neighbouring countries, notably Liberia and Guinea. The three member states of the Mano River Union (MRU)—Guinea, Liberia and Sierra Leone—will have to harmonize their national legislation on corruption and arms regulation. It is imperative that the establishment of joint security commissions and joint border patrols follows this initial institutional step. This will contribute greatly to preventing the recycling of weapons and illegal transfers and trafficking from one country to another.

In the fight against arms-related corruption, the West African moratorium on small arms and light weapons[43] is an important first step, pointing the way to regional cooperation. The fact remains, however, that, until it is included in the legal framework of each member state, the moratorium is only a morally binding document. Common legal constraints are required on both sides of national frontiers if we want to curb the proliferation of small arms and light weapons—and the corruption and insecurity they engender—throughout West Africa.

CONCLUSION

Arms trafficking is flourishing. Since they have power and money—two precious assets for corruption—it is easy for arms traffickers to corrupt weak governments. For four decades, Sierra Leone has been a weak and highly corrupted state.[44] The outcome of policies aimed at curbing the proliferation of small arms and light weapons in Sierra Leone depends largely on what happens in the fight against corruption. An ineffective anti-corruption strategy will lead to ineffective control of small arms and light weapons proliferation.[45]

The government cannot succeed on its own. Effective anti-corruption and anti-small arms proliferation policies demand a holistic approach, in which civil society and community-based organizations play an important support role. Combating corruption has elements common to every society: it requires methods for assuring accountability, changes in moral and ethical attitudes, and, perhaps most importantly, the combined involvement of government, moral and religious leaders, the private business sector and civil society.[46] This point was illustrated by Dieter Frische, former Director-General of Development at the European Commission, when he observed that "corruption raises the cost of goods to services; it increases the debt of a country (and carries with it rearing debt-servicing costs in the future); it leads to lowering of standards, as sub-standard goods are provided and inappropriate or unnecessary technology is acquired; and it results in project choices being made based on capital (because it is more rewarding for the perpetrator of corruption) than on manpower, which would be the more useful for development."[47]

Sierra Leone should follow the example of other countries in sub-Saharan Africa in challenging corruption. To succeed, we must provide civic training for public servants coupled with adequate remuneration, and introduce new standards of decentralized participatory governance. But in Sierra Leone, the anti-corruption drive will succeed only if it deals with diamonds. Diamond smuggling must be discouraged at all levels: this also calls for responsibility from multinational firms like de Beers and Executive Outcomes, and the Western governments that have the power to influence their behaviour. For it is not just corrupt politicians and soldiers who have caused corruption to bloom in Sierra Leone: the contribution of the illegal diamond trade to war and corruption has been immense.[48]

Notes

1   Ian Smillie, Lansana Gberie and Ralph Hazleton, *The Heart of the Matter: Sierra Leone, Diamonds, and Human Security*, Ontario: Partnership Africa Canada Publication, January 2000, p. 5.

2   UNDP, *Sierra Leone Human Development Report*, New York and Freetown: United Nations, April 1999, p. 18.

3   See, for instance, Paul M. Heywood and Paul Haywood (eds), *Political Corruption*, London: Blackwell, 1997.

4   Susan Rose-Ackerman, *Corruption and Government: Causes, Consequences and Reforms*, Cambridge: Cambridge University Press, 1999; Kimberly Elliott (ed.), *Corruption and the Global Economy*, Institute for International Economics, 1997; Mark Robinson (ed.), *Corruption and Development*, Frank Cass Publications, 1998; Robin Theobald, *Corruption, Development and Underdevelopment*, Duke University Press, 1999.

5   Jeremy Pope, *National Integrity Systems: Transparency International Source Book*, Berlin, April 1997, p. 1.

6   Paul Richards, *Fighting for the Rainforest: War, Youth and Resources in Sierra Leone*, London: Villiers Publications, 1996, p. 9.

7   "Villains or Redeemers", *NewBreed*, Freetown: 13 October 1993, p. 2.

8   *NPRC Commissions of Inquiry Reports*, Freetown: Government Printing Press, October 1994, pp. 89–107.

9   Jimmy Kande, "Politicisation of Ethnic Identities in Sierra Leone", *African Studies Review*, Vol. 35, No. 1, 1992, pp. 81–89.

10 The Arms and Ammunition Ordinance Act of 1955, Part 3, Section 8.

11 Ibid., Section 19.

12 T. M. Lahun, Department Headquarters, Economic Crime Syndicate Criminal Investigations, Freetown, 14 November 1999.

13 The Constitution of Sierra Leone, 1991.

14 James Chowning Davies, *When Men Revolt and Why*, New York: The Free Press, 1971, pp. 260–281.

15 Paul Richards, op. cit., p. 26.

16 Ibid., p. 22.

17 Ibid.

18 See Johan Peleman, "Mining for Serious Trouble: Jean-Raymond Boulle and His Corporate Empire Project", in Abdel-Fatau Musah and J. Kayode Fayemi (eds), *Mercenaries. An African Security Dilemma*, London: Pluto Press, 2000, pp. 155–168.

19 Edward J. Laurance, *Light Weapons and Intrastate Conflict*, Washington, DC: Carnegie Corporation, 1998, pp. 31–32.

20 Jakkie Cilliers and Peggy Mason (eds), *Peace, Profit or Plunder? The Privatisation of Security in War-Torn African Societies*, Pretoria: Institute for Security Studies, 1999.

21 *Quarterly Journal of the Center for Democracy and Development*, Vol. 2, No 1 and 2, January–June 1999, p. 11.

22 Ibid., p. 12.

23 Ibid. See also Abdel-Fatau Musah and J. Kayode Fayemi (eds), *Mercenaries. An African Security Dilemma*, London: Pluto Press, 2000.

24 *Quarterly Journal of the Center for Democracy and Development*, op. cit., pp. 13–14.

25 Paul Richards, op. cit., p. 13.

26 *Standard Times*, Freetown, 23 August 1999, p. 1.

27 *New Breed Press*, Freetown, 13 October 1993, p. 4.

28 *Quarterly Journal of the Center for Democracy and Development*, op. cit., p. 23.

29 *Concord Times*, Freetown, 10 September 1998, p. 1.

30 *Standard Times*, Freetown, 14 September 1999, p. 2.

[31] *Standard Times*, Freetown, 14 September 1999, p. 3.

[32] *For di People*, Freetown, 24 November 1999, p. 1.

[33] *Independent Observer*, Freetown, 22 September 1999, p. 1.

[34] *Concord Times*, Freetown, 10 June 1997, p. 3.

[35] *For di People*, Freetown, 24 November 1999, p.1.

[36] *Standard Times*, Freetown, 14 September 1999, p. 2.

[37] See *The Long Road to Peace: Report of National Consultative Process in Sierra Leone*, Freetown: Chriskal Printing Enterprises, 1999.

[38] *Concord Times*, Freetown, 10 June 1997, p. 3.

[39] See <www.sierra-leone.org>, March–April 1999.

[40] *Independent Observer*, Freetown, 22 September 1999, p. 1.

[41] *For di People*, Freetown, 23 November 1999, p. 2.

[42] Anti-Corruption Act, 1999, Part II, Section 3.

[43] The Declaration of a Moratorium on the Importation, Exportation and Manufacture of Small Arms and Light Weapons in West Africa was signed by the 16 heads of government of ECOWAS on 31 October 1998. The moratorium entered into force the next day, 1 November. For more information on the moratorium see Jacqueline Seck, *West Africa Small Arms Moratorium: High-Level Consultations on the Modalities for the Implementation of PCASED*, Geneva: United Nations, 2000.

[44] William Reno, *Corruption and State Politics in Sierra Leone*, Cambridge: Cambridge University Press, 1995.

[45] On policies aiming at improving integrity and transparency in government see, for instance, Sahr J. Kpundeh, "Political Will: The Core of Anti-Corruption Reform", communication to a joint OECD, OSCE and World Bank conference in Paris, 15–16 July 1998.

[46] G. Shabbir Cheema (ed.), *Good Governance and Corruption*, Diane Publishing Company, 1999.

[47] As quoted in *Concord Times*, Freetown, 18 February 2000, p. 1.

[48] See Ian Smillie, Lansana Gberie and Ralph Hazleton, op. cit.

CHAPTER 7

PEACE BY OTHER MEANS:
THE MISSING LINK IN DDR PROGRAMMES

Michael Foray

WHAT WENT WRONG: THE POLITICS OF BAD GOVERNANCE

> Peace with dignity. Peace with commitment. This is our
> gift to our peoples and the generations to come. It will be
> real, as we open our hearts and minds to each other.
> **King Hussein of Jordan**[1]

There are many things about Sierra Leone's nine-year civil war that can be accurately described as unique. Unlike civil wars in other parts of Africa, the traditional antagonisms of religious strife, tribal and ethnic tensions, ancient feuds and historical hatred between groups of people are not major factors in Sierra Leone's civil conflict. Yet the war in Sierra Leone ranks among the most gruesome conflicts the twentieth century has known in its long, violent history.[2] The unrelenting terror to which the people of Sierra Leone have been subjected over the war years has included gang rape, abduction, maiming, amputation, burning and wanton murder of innocent people, including infants and the aged. Even as hopes are pinned on an ever-shifting horizon of peace, the question persists: what went wrong?

As we chart the way forward, the question is pertinent, because, once upon a time, Sierra Leoneans were well described as peace-loving, hospitable people. Many still are; but so much has happened, so much has been lost, so much is still going on, that no one really knows any longer what "peace" is.

The country was and is still blessed with fertile land and an abundance of natural resources, including diamonds, gold, iron, bauxite and rutile. In spite of its natural wealth, the country did not have to fight for independence. The terms of Sierra Leone's independence were set at a constitutional conference in Lancaster House, London, in April and May 1960.[3] In the years immediately after independence in 1961, Sierra Leone continued to flourish under a Westminster-style parliamentary democracy. The rule of law prevailed. Administrative structures inherited from over half a century of British colonial rule continued to serve the country. Sierra Leone enjoys the singular distinction of being the first country in black Africa to have a university, and was sometimes described as "the Athens of West Africa". For years Sierra Leone enjoyed strong friendships with all its neighbours, and with countries in the subregion and beyond.

The events of the last nine years have crippled the economy, redefined the polity, and put our very humanity at risk. For Sierra Leone to survive and recover from this rebel war it must have real peace, and this will not come easily. The war itself is not the root of the problem. It is merely the appalling symptom of a much deeper distress, which festered during almost three decades of bad politics, ineptitude and banditry in the public service, much which still goes on. The conditions and events that preceded the war, whether causative, associative or unrelated to the barbarity and horror of this conflict, must be understood and accounted for in any permanent peace solution.

This is, however, yet to happen through the institutions of government and its international partners. Among the many reasons for this is the singular focus on the political leadership of the rebel movement, to the exclusion of the rebel foot soldiers and the many victims of the war. There is also excessive reliance on band-aid approaches to disarmament and demobilization, and mere lip service paid to reintegration.

The traditional government-managed approaches to peace are narrowly conceived, stereotypical, and partial to the interests of a government that is very much a part of the problem. Resource limitations are significant, but they are not the determining factor. The financial resources committed to the Sierra Leone peace process by the international community thus far would be more than adequate to put the process on a solid course to permanent and lasting peace. But they must be deployed optimally: and that is yet to happen.

For these reasons, the rural people who bear the brunt of the war, the members of the Civil Defence Forces (CDF) who put their lives on the line to defend them, and the rebel soldiers who fight and die for promised benefits (of which they will never partake), must together seek people- and community-based solutions.

The political leaderships of Africa's governments and rebel movements will, if given the choice between people and power, choose the latter. Like those before them, political power and control of the resources of the state, not the demonstrated ability to make things better, are the hallmarks of leadership. That is very much how we reached this precipice of chaos and disaster. The leadership class—political, business, professional and otherwise—failed over the years to serve the interests of the people of Sierra Leone. The political leadership and their business partners exploited and corrupted the country, and when they fell out of favour they raised armies of thugs to subdue the population by violent means.

The worst of these transgressions occurred under the All People's Congress (APC) party, from 1968 to 1992. In the process of perpetuating and enriching itself, the APC, under both Siaka Stevens and Joseph Momoh, subverted the rule of law, undermined public institutions, popularized and institutionalized a culture of violence and corruption. The civil service and the judiciary were deeply corrupted, the army and the police were politicized and the economy was criminalized and destroyed. In short, the whole moral fabric of society was completely shredded.[4]

In 1973, for example, the elections conducted by the APC were marred by such unbridled violence that the rival Sierra Leone People's Party (SLPP) withdrew in fear and in protest. Their move gave the APC complete control of Parliament. It wasted no time in enacting laws designed to suppress opposition and retain power. The country regressed and the people were impoverished. The social, economic and political conditions ideal for violent rebellion fomented. In 1977, students mounted a nationwide protest that forced the APC to dissolve Parliament and go to the polls. Anarchy and destruction spread across the country: anger was expressed by people way beyond the student community. Government officials, assets and institutions were targeted. With hindsight we can see that, in 1977, the population was giving a first glimpse of the rage within.

The APC government ignored the warning signs and capitalized on the emergency situation in the country to strengthen its grip on power further. APC candidates brutalized and intimidated political opponents, burnt and vandalized private property, and established a hitherto unimagined tyranny over a once peaceful nation. The tyranny continued unchallenged until the late 1980s, when political and economic conditions became increasingly intolerable. The frustrations of Sierra Leonean dissidents in Liberia and the rest of the world, marginalized political hardliners at home, revolutionary university students and academics, unemployed urban youth and peasants, were the seeds in a muddled ferment in which the Revolutionary United Front (RUF) germinated and sprang to life.

THE REBEL WAR AND REBEL PEACE

Political aspirants capitalized on widespread disgruntlement, fuelled a rebellion with arms and mercenaries, and distressed the population to the point of displacing over forty per cent of the people. Diamonds attracted unscrupulous business interests, complicating the problem and compounding the crisis. Political and socio-economic mismanagement was transformed into a violent armed crisis, which continues to shock the world.

In 1992, one year after the RUF started its war, junior military officers succeeded in overthrowing the government of Joseph Momoh. Many Sierra Leoneans at home and abroad welcomed the change; but the junta fell out of favour thanks to corruption, excesses and a failure to bring the war to an end. In 1995 a palace coup resulted in a change of leadership within the junta, from Captain Valentine Strasser to Brigadier Julius Maada Bio. The latter negotiated a ceasefire with the RUF in December 1995. Under international pressure and calls for democracy at home, the junta conducted elections, which brought the current government of Ahmad Tejan Kabbah to power in 1996.

Since 1996, Sierra Leone has attempted several peace negotiations, which have brought the Abidjan Peace Accord and the Lomé Accord. The war intensified as each agreement failed. At the time of writing, one year after the Lomé Accord was signed on 7 July 1999, a full-term foetus seems to be in the throes of birth. The birth pangs have been prolonged; the baby of peace is not yet born, and much can still go very wrong. If the Lomé peace process follows the model of its predecessors, we can expect blood, putting the mother and all her other children at risk.

The peace agreement and its official implementation plan will not resolve the problems of this country alone. Expectations are unrealistic. A small, ad hoc National Commission for Disarmament, Demobilization and Reintegration (NCDDR) is expected to rehabilitate over 45,000 ex-combatants and reintegrate them into society as productive citizens. There is no coordinated national programme for long-term reconstruction. Over half a million people, known to be displaced and afflicted by the war, are largely uncatered for. The conditions of poverty and alienation that precipitated the war persist, and are probably worse than before the war. The government, which should lead Sierra Leone out of this quagmire, has barely been able to hold on to power, and has had to be reinstated by foreign forces twice in twelve months.

The official approach to the Sierra Leone peace process focuses on disarming, demobilizing and reintegrating fighting forces. The underlying causes of the war, and the fighters in the field, are ignored, neglected or badly handled. The Lomé Peace Accord addresses the aspirations of the political leadership of the rebel movement to the point of creating political offices and specifying the political appointments they will receive. Implementation focuses on disarming and disbanding rebel fighters with the cooperation of the rebel leaders: the fighters are expected to be satisfied with promises of reintegration benefits, which are vaguely defined, experimental at best, and demonstrably beyond the capacity of a government that is ineffective to begin with. If expectations are created that will not be fulfilled, and if social and economic conditions continue along present trends, this war will not end with peace and disarmament, even if DDR is one hundred per cent successful.

LOOKING WITHIN

Internal solutions that address underlying causes of crises are important to the process. Sierra Leone's problems pre-date 1991, when the war started. Political violence, economic deprivation, unfettered corruption and the imminent failure of the nation state are pre-war phenomena. The efforts of the international community, while considerable and well intentioned, have still only succeeded in propping up governments that would otherwise collapse. It is time to look within. It is in this context and within this logic that the Movement to Unite People (MUP), a locally based Sierra Leonean non-governmental organization, contributes to peace endeavours and reconciliation processes at the grass-roots level.

MOTIVES AND METHODS

The Movement to Unite People focuses on a grass-roots intervention strategy predicated on personal and community interests, and demonstrates how these are best achieved in an atmosphere of peace and progress. Methods include individual and group discussions, meetings and workshops, during which issues are addressed from individual and community perspectives. People want food on their tables, clothes on their backs, a roof over their heads, a future for their children, and general progress in their lives. No one achieves these things by destroying life and property. The idea is simple enough. However, the events of the last few decades demonstrate otherwise. A generation of young people has been robbed of opportunity, alienated from families and communities, and simply disinherited. Today they have nothing and nowhere to go. If they are given leadership, they are ready to follow. The Movement to Unite People intervenes to lead them from a path of death and destruction to a path to peace and progress. After "disarmament", these young people need to be helped to find themselves a new life, which is not supported by violence and abuse of the gun.

Combatants need to be assured that they will be able to live safely and peacefully in the communities against which they have committed terrible atrocities. People and communities throughout Sierra Leone, bereaved and aggrieved by the atrocities committed against them, and largely neglected in the peace process, must give combatants these assurances. This is the core of the MUP programme. We call it peace consolidation at combatant and community level.

These young people are victims as much as they are perpetrators. Some were abducted and forcibly inducted into rebel ranks, others joined voluntarily to change their lives. Many rebel soldiers are still children, taken from their villages at as young as five or six years of age. Not all are immediately salvageable; but the majority are desperate to be rescued from a violent life of alienation, hopelessness and despair. This is where the process must begin.

REPENTANCE AND ASSURANCE

Addressing the apprehension that many combatants feel about living in communities and among people they have traumatized and victimized during the course of this war is a precondition for unreserved disarmament, full demobilization and safe reintegration. So the Movement to Unite People goes into villages and towns and talks to people. The war is put in perspective. Rebels could be anyone's son or daughter. This is not the life many would have lived in a society with security and opportunity. Now the nation must move forward, and it cannot do so if some are set on revenge, determined to alienate ex-combatants and be generally hostile and uncompromising. If ex-combatants cannot find a place in the villages and towns of Sierra Leone as neighbours, they may end up in the bush as enemies. And there will be no peace.

Rebels must also express and demonstrate a commitment to peace. They must express remorse and ask the communities for forgiveness. MUP seeks rebels, wherever they are, and explains its programme. A reconciliation process is the only way forward in the peace process, using the African tradition of engaging elders, senior family members, religious leaders, and respected members of communities to intercede on behalf of transgressors. Fear of retribution is an obstacle to true and lasting peace. If combatants are afraid and communities are distrustful, the peace will remain tenuous. The intervention and involvement of MUP at community and combatant levels throughout Sierra Leone is a necessary corollary to the political process started in Togo.

The MUP programme anticipates the difficulties that individual combatants may experience in reintegration. These may include simple everyday problems such as renting a place to live, getting a job, making new friendships and settling into a new environment. Combatants are cautioned against attributing any problems they encounter to their rebel past. Most importantly, they should not react in ways that would make people fearful and apprehensive of having ex-combatants in their homes and neighbourhoods, in their schools and businesses, and among their children. Respected community members are recruited to act as counsellors: they can provide an outlet for frustration, give advice and use their influence in the community to help ex-combatants along the road to integration.

Meeting the People

The first MUP field trip was to Port Loko and Lunsar. The former was under the Economic Community of West African States Monitoring Group (ECOMOG) control and the latter was under rebel control. It was a tense time, and coincided with the abduction of ECOMOG and UNOMSIL (United Nations Observer Mission in Sierra Leone) officers by rebels at the infamous Okra Hill (in early August 1999, just one month after the signing ceremony in Lomé). MUP was the first organization to bring the Lomé Accord to rebel-occupied areas of the country.

The goal of the trip was to consolidate peace at the grass roots. This was achieved by engaging communities and combatants in dialogue. Six members of the Movement travelled by road to Port Loko and met with the Chief and community leaders. The programme was explained first to the Chief and his council of elders, who gave their blessing and prayed for the success of the programme. A second meeting was held in the town court with community leaders, including pastors, teachers, imams, traders and farmers. The Movement recorded the leaders' commitments to the peace programme on audio and videotape. The community leaders undertook to provide land for ex-combatants to farm and build homes, and wives for them to marry and start families.

The Movement then proceeded to Lunsar, where it was well received by RUF rebels. The story was retold, and the commanders heard the audiotapes from Port Loko. They agreed to ask the communities throughout Sierra Leone for their forgiveness and committed themselves to full participation in the peace consolidation programme proposed by the Movement.

A town meeting was held in Lunsar, in which traditional rulers, community leaders and the townspeople were all present, among RUF commanders and fighters. The Movement explained its programme and asked for commitments. The people gave their commitments, and the RUF asked for their forgiveness. In the true African tradition, the entire community acted as one family and for Lunsar the *palava* was settled. Community leaders undertook to continue the work started by the movement. The RUF commanders conceded that not all their members could be relied upon in consolidating the peace process. They stated, however, that the RUF in Lunsar was weary of war and wanted to work with the people to rebuild the country and prosper in peace. They pointed out that since the previous May, when the ceasefire was signed, the RUF in Lunsar had prohibited all its members from firing their weapons, even to hunt for meat. They cited this—and the prosecution of RUF members who violated the ceasefire—as evidence of their commitment to peace. They reiterated their commitment to peace, asked the people to forgive and accept them as their sons and daughters, echoing the theme that *"Bad bush nor dae for troway bad pikin"*, a Krio proverb, which translates to: "There is no bad place to dispose of bad children".

BEYOND DISARMAMENT

The activities of MUP go beyond sensitization. Without disarmament there can be no peace; but once people have been persuaded to lay down their arms, they must be given a vision of hope, an impression of economic and social progress. There are massive economic and social problems for which viable solutions have not even been proposed. Thousands of homes have been destroyed, lives lost, women widowed, children orphaned, communities scattered, businesses abandoned and economies crippled by nine years of killing, looting and burning. If low income, unemployment, and the availability of housing, education and opportunity were problems in 1991, when this war started, today they are a way of life.

FOUR WALLS AND A ROOF

The Movement to Unite People has presented a draft proposal to the Ministry of Housing for a project called Four Walls and a Roof. It is a housing concept for low-income families in Sierra Leone. The idea is to help replace some of the homes destroyed during the war and create employment by building safe and affordable housing in rural and urban communities.

The concept goes beyond a roof over one's head. It is conceived of as an economic development tool tied to a private sector- and community-based delivery mechanism, including a national housing finance superstructure. The housing industry is critical to post-war reconstruction and development, because it is extensively linked to other economic sectors. It stimulates growth and economic activity, and it is labour intensive. All the materials required are locally produced, except for imported wire nails, which are a minute component. The potential of the project for putting large numbers of people to work in construction, transportation, timber production, finance, sales and management is considerable. The role of the Ministry of Housing will be to create an enabling environment for the growth of the industry, the organization and working of the construction economy, and to coordinate the sector's role in national reconstruction and development. Initial estimates put the cost of each base unit, excluding land (which is expected to come from central and local government land grants), at about one thousand dollars. Ten thousand units costing a total of ten million dollars are proposed initially. The project will stimulate growth in transport, food production, tools, timber, sand, stone and brick production, provide direct employment for thousands of skilled and unskilled workers, supervisors and managers, as well as a market for a range of services. It will also complement other development initiatives by providing a mechanism for relocating displaced populations, reintegrating and employing ex-combatants, while supporting agriculture, fishing and mining projects.

FORMER CHILD SOLDIERS AT RISK

The MUP organization has developed a post-encampment reintegration support programme for child soldiers and young adult combatants (those in the high teens), and is currently seeking funding for its implementation. The programme uses a community-based mechanism for the sensitization and socio-economic rehabilitation of child combatants over 15 years old. This group is considered high risk, because neither traditional foster care nor adult reintegration programmes are fully appropriate or adapted to their unique needs. Child combatants in this age bracket in Sierra Leone often share the following characteristics, giving rise to unique needs.

- They were abducted at a very early age and have been in combat for several years.
- As a result of this interruption in the most formative period of their lives, they have lost, or never developed, useful social, educational and economic skills, and it may be too late for them to integrate into the normal school and social learning system.
- They have a reputation as dangerous soldiers because they have survived. As a result they elicit fear and apprehension from members of their communities.

- These factors are mutually reinforcing, and militate against their acceptance into communities, therefore threatening the success of socio-economic reintegration programmes.

For these reasons, the Movement to Unite People proposes a programme for rehabilitating child combatants over 15 to facilitate their reintegration into host communities.

The programme concept is adapted from the "community agent theory" used to address unsatisfactory and hostile relations between inner city schools in the United States and the ghetto communities they serve. The theory is based on the premise that a child cannot be adequately educated without considering all the forces that play on that child. The sociologist Harold Taylor[5] refers to the "whole child" in discussing education as a total process in which the conditions of society deeply affect a child's mind, their level of achievement and range of possibilities. The adaptation of this theory focuses on community involvement and social action, interaction and intervention by community agents in a liaison capacity between the child combatant and the host community. Intervention devices will include:

- Activities like sport, drama, music, culture, vocational training, etc. to occupy the child, provide a controlled medium of interaction with other members of the community and generally contract the time available to engage in deviant conduct.
- Community service and developmental activities like tree planting, cleaning, facilities development and maintenance, etc. to inculcate public spiritedness in the child and give a sense of worth and belonging to the host community.
- Career counselling, mentorship and guidance for successful transition into productive adult life.
- Economic project development and management to provide part-time or full-time jobs for target beneficiaries as well as their contemporaries in the host community. This exercise is aimed at developing work ethics, reinforcing a sense of self-worth and teaching the child how to make an honest living, as well as breed a sense of oneness with other children in host communities.

The sensitization of target beneficiaries shall be integrated into a learned behavioural approach, wherein the lessons of responsible and productive social life are lived. Rehabilitation itself is conceived as a realized experience into which the child graduates. Reintegration and social acceptance shall be demonstrated by doing things with the community and for the benefit of the community. Contribution to and acceptance by the host community shall determine the success of the programme in transforming the child soldier at risk into a respected and responsible member of society.

CONCLUSION

These programmes, and much of what the Movement to Unite People does, must be understood in the context of expectation and outcome. The approach is premised on the scientific evidence that a manifest belief in human potential is necessary to the development process that one wishes to inspire. The attitudes that a worker has toward the people he or she works with, that a teacher has toward students, or that a parent has toward a child, contribute substantially to their development or lack thereof. The expectations implicit in the programmes and activities are therefore critical to the rehabilitation strategy and peace consolidation objective.

MUP programmes and initiatives are optimistic about people's potential for development, and seek to excite initiative and confidence in others. For the programmes to succeed, they must help people discover abilities and good impulses that they may not be aware they possess. These abilities and impulses will emerge and strengthen when people work together in groups that serve the common (community) good. It is hoped that the satisfaction and self-confidence gained from small accomplishments will develop the confidence and ability to contend with more difficult problems in a continuous process of perpetual self-guided growth.

Notes

1   Declaration made on 27 October 1994 at a peace negotiation meeting with Israeli Prime Minister Yitzhak Rabin near the Gulf of Aqaba.
2   On conflict and violence in the twentieth century, see Eric J. Hobsbawm, *The Age of Extremes: A History of the World, 1914–1991,*

New York: Vintage Books, 1996; Jonathan Glover, *Humanity. A Moral History of the Twentieth Century*, London: Jonathan Cape, 1999.

3   For the details of modern Sierra Leonean history, see Joe A. D. Alie, *A New History of Sierra Leone*, London: Macmillan, 1990.

4   William Reno, *Corruption and State Politics in Sierra Leone*, Cambridge: Cambridge University Press, 1995.

5   Harold Taylor, *The World as Teacher*, Southern Illinois University Press, 1974.

CHAPTER 8

DISARMAMENT, DEMOBILIZATION AND REINTEGRATION IN POST-WAR SIERRA LEONE

Francis Kai-Kai

Sierra Leone has been embroiled in a brutal civil war ever since the incursion of the Revolutionary United Front (RUF) in March 1991 from neighbouring Liberia. During this period, the country has witnessed some of the worst violations of human rights and humanitarian law in the world. One of the most alarming trends in the armed conflict is the abduction and recruitment of children, young men and women who are forced to fight and work with the rebel forces. Following the restoration of democracy in February 1998 the Government of Sierra Leone embarked on a policy to end the conflict and pursue peace and reconciliation. The Lomé Peace Agreement was eventually signed between the government and the RUF on 7 July 1999. The agreement provided the framework for a ceasefire, governance and peace-building after many years of war. The disarmament, demobilization and reintegration (DDR) programme was conceived within this framework. The government became committed to the complete disarmament, demobilization and reintegration of an estimated 45,000 combatants.

OVERVIEW OF THE DDR PROGRAMME

OBJECTIVES

Ex-combatants constitute a considerable risk group, which is capable of undermining any security gains in Sierra Leone. They therefore require special attention and targeted assistance. In the short term, the security benefits of the disarmament and demobilization exercise have a financial cost, incurred in facilitating the return of the combatants to normal civilian life. The Government of Sierra Leone is determined to ensure that the planned disarmament and demobilization of combatants is made socially and politically viable by putting in place a comprehensive reintegration programme.

Thus, the goal of the disarmament, demobilization and reintegration programme is the consolidation of existing short-term security to form the basis for lasting peace. The overall programme aims to:

- collect, register, destroy and dispose of all conventional weapons and ammunition retrieved from the combatants during the disarmament process;
- demobilize approximately 45,000 combatants, comprising the following factions: Sierra Leone Army (SLA)–6,000, Armed Forces Revolutionary Council (AFRC)–7,000, RUF–15,000, Civil Defence Forces (CDF)–15,000, and paramilitary forces as designated in the Lomé Agreement–2,000. Disabled and child combatants constitute approximately twelve per cent of the total number of combatants to be demobilized, and require special reintegration support; and
- prepare for the sustainable social and economic reintegration of all ex-combatants for long-term security.

On the basis of these objectives, a comprehensive strategic framework has been developed for all programme activities, covering expected results, performance indicators and benchmarks.

PROGRAMME PRINCIPLES AND ASSUMPTIONS

For the DDR programme to be meaningful and contribute to security and lasting peace, it was clear that it had to establish certain principles and assumptions. Some of these principles include:

- Simultaneous and parallel implementation of a comprehensive plan for the restructuring of the national army together with the DDR programme. This will be done by the Ministry of Defence, which is drawing up a military reintegration plan with the help of experts provided by the British government.[1]
- Representation of all erstwhile fighting groups on the National Committee for Disarmament, Demobilization and Reintegration.

These groups are equally entitled to benefit from similar assistance from the programme.

Prior to demobilization, the government will undertake a well-planned sensitization campaign to educate the general public about the programme and the role of ex-combatants in a post-conflict society.

Some assumptions were also made.

- Peacekeeping forces, that is, the Economic Community of West African States Monitoring Group (ECOMOG) and the United Nations Mission in Sierra Leone (UNAMSIL), will provide security within the framework of their revised mandates and new rules of engagement as specified by Article XV of the Lomé Agreement.
- The required number of UNAMSIL observers with necessary logistics will arrive and be deployed in time to operationalize disarmament sites and demobilization centres around the country along with ECOMOG.
- Compliance and adherence by all parties to the relevant provisions of the Lomé Peace Agreement, especially those pertaining to the DDR programme.
- The parties' willingness and capacity to deliver combatants and weapons to the areas designated for each party.
- The international community will assist the government and the peace process by mobilizing funds for the DDR programme.

THE INSTITUTIONAL FRAMEWORK

A robust institutional framework is required to implement a programme aiming at DDR. Recognizing the immensity of this task, the government has established linkages with a number of institutions at local, national and international levels. The key players within this configuration include the government, the peacekeeping forces—ECOMOG and UNAMSIL, the United Nations agencies, the United Kingdom Department for International Development, the World Bank, a number of non-governmental organizations and the high command of the erstwhile fighting forces. The government, with the support of the international community, set up a National Committee for Disarmament, Demobilization and Reintegration (NCDDR). The NCDDR brings together all the stakeholders in the peace process, including the leaders of the different factions in the war, the peacekeeping forces and representatives of donors. The head of state is the chair of the Committee.

An Executive Secretariat has been established to implement the policies of the National Committee within the framework of a national DDR programme. The Executive Secretariat has its headquarters in Freetown, with regional offices in the Eastern, Northern and Southern Provinces and the Western Area. For coordination of implementation, the Secretariat has instituted Technical Coordination Committees.

The first of these committees focuses on disarmament and demobilization issues, including operational difficulties and procedures and special approaches to child ex-combatants. The committee meets on a weekly basis. The membership of this committee includes all those in charge of operations: UNAMSIL, the United Nations Children's Fund (UNICEF), the Sierra Leonean ministry responsible for children, and the child protection agencies. The different ex-fighting factions are also represented on the committee.

The other Technical Coordination Committee focuses on the reintegration of the ex-combatants, including children. This body brings together a larger number of government institutions, United Nations agencies and non-governmental organizations involved in the implementation of various aspects of social and economic reintegration of former combatants. Coordination of reintegration assistance is also closely linked to the overall coordination of resettlement and rehabilitation of internally displaced persons and refugees.

As well as providing the institutional framework for coordination, the government has assigned specific roles to the different stakeholders in the implementation of the DDR programme. UNAMSIL is responsible for disarmament, which is essentially a military activity. It provides security for the entire peace process and ensures the protection of the rights of the disarmed ex-combatants. UNICEF has been mandated to coordinate all the agencies active in child welfare. This is being done within the ambit of the child protection network, under the direction of the Ministry of Gender and Children's Affairs. These agencies implement child-focused programmes and play a major role in child demobilization at interim care centres and also in their eventual reintegration into their families and communities. Other international agencies have been contracted to carry out specific tasks such as setting up and assisting in the administration of demobilization centres.

PROGRAMME IMPLEMENTATION

Implementation of DDR is multi-staged, with activities carried out in three different locations. Disarmament activities take place at reception centres: ex-combatants are assembled, weapons and ammunition collected, and interviews are held. Weapon collection, storage and destruction are particularly important in the disarmament process in Sierra Leone. Weapons, once collected, are disabled by the removal of their working parts and their separation from the rest of the frame. These are stored in separate containers, which are held in separate locations, away from the demobilization and reception centres. The storage centres are protected by peacekeepers. Table 1 summarizes the number of ex-combatants disarmed since the inception of the DDR programme and the accompanying weapons and ammunition collected before the current impasse.

A number of reception centres are associated with a single demobilization centre. At the demobilization centres, various activities take place to assist the ex-combatants commence their transition to civilian life. The activities include screening, reintegration and expectations interviews, and preparation to re-enter home communities. A major part of the preparation is the referral of under-age combatants and other children to child protection agencies. The ex-combatants are further prepared for civilian life by the implementation of pre-discharge orientation activities and the provision of transportation and transitional safety allowances to support them during the first three months of their return to their home communities.

The final stage of the process is reintegration, and this takes place at the community level. Most ex-combatants feel uprooted at this stage, without a regular source of income to meet the basic challenges of life. Some are not able to adjust socially, either because of past rebel activities or estrangement from their own communities after years of absence. Therefore, the six months immediately following discharge from the demobilization centres are envisaged as the most challenging for many ex-combatants (especially the RUF).

Table 1: Summary of combatants disarmed and weapons collected in Sierra Leone's DDR programme

Category	Target	Disarmed	% of target disarmed
RUF	15,000	4,503	30
AFRC/ex-SLA	7,000	5,771	82
Current/Loyal SLA	6,000	3,804	63
CDF	15,000	8,744	58
Others (inc. discharged SLA)	2,000	1,463	73
Total	**45,000**	**24,285**	**54**

Children	Adults
1,743	22,542

Weapons	Number collected
Assorted (ex-Kabala)	135
AK-47	4,224
AK-58	1,061
FN rifle	413
SAR	447
G-III	924
LMG	140
RPG-7	217
Mortar	45
Others	2,742
Hand grenades	1,856
Pistols	493
Pre 4 Nov 1999	141
Assorted (discharged SLA)	1,969
Total*	**14,807**

Ammunition	
Ammunition	254,565
Pre 4 Nov 1999	1,154
Total*	**255,719**
* The figures do not include weapons and ammunition collected from loyal SLA which are now stored in armoury and magazines.	

Source: M & E Unit, Executive Secretariat of the NCDDR, UNAMSIL, and ECOMOG, May 2000.

In order to facilitate the transition of the members of each group to civilian life, the NCDDR has planned to provide each adult ex-combatant with a monetized settling-in package in the form of transitional safety allowances (TSA) of US$ 300. This is calculated on the basis of a basket of basic needs (food, shelter, health, education, tools and seeds) that an average family needs to survive in Sierra Leone. Adult ex-combatants will receive the first instalment before leaving the demobilization centres. They will then be eligible to receive one further instalment in their district headquarters, three months after discharge. The payment of this safety net is spaced in order to provide ex-combatants with an incentive to remain in their district of settlement, and to prevent irresponsible allocation of resources immediately after demobilization. Such a modality will also inject resources into rural, war-affected areas. Verification of ex-combatant status for the receipt of the second instalment will be effected by way of the non-transferable identity card each ex-combatant will receive during demobilization.

Given the fact that the majority of ex-combatants have neither completed their formal education nor acquired marketable skills, the economic outlook for most of them is bleak. Absorption in the formal sector, including the civil service, is beyond the reach of unskilled or illiterate ex-combatants. Hence the need to offer options for economic reintegration, in particular in agriculture and the informal sector. This will hopefully avoid the need for ex-combatants to revert to rent seeking behind the barrel of a gun. The following activities have been deliberately targeted at ex-combatants.

- The provision of information, counselling and referral services at the regional and district level, which will provide ex-combatants with information about potential opportunities for employment, participation in the private sector and community-based national reconstruction and rehabilitation activities.
- An employment, vocational training and apprenticeship fund, known as the regional Training and Employment Fund, would provide ex-combatants with access to apprenticeships or vocational training and would subsidize employment opportunities where possible.

For ex-combatants who wish to settle in rural areas, the Executive Secretariat, in coordination with the National Commission for Reconstruction, Resettlement and Rehabilitation, would liaise with relevant chiefdom and district authorities to encourage reconciliation and to facilitate access to land where possible.

The essence of economic reintegration assistance is (1) to link training to employment; (2) to be geared to the training needs of the ex-combatants, that is, to be demand driven; and (3) to help stimulate the creation of new training and employment provision, through the input of funds and demand. Overall, economic reintegration assistance aims to provide ex-combatants with opportunities to acquire and employ marketable skills to enable them to lead gainful and productive lives and to contribute to the development of their communities.

Former child combatants are also provided for through specialized agencies, such as UNICEF and other child protection agencies, to facilitate their reinsertion and reintegration.

CHALLENGES TO THE DDR PROGRAMME

The DDR programme, like the overall peace process in the country, has faced many constraints since implementation commenced. At every stage, adjustments have been necessary to ensure that the programme does not stall. However, until the recent resumption of hostilities by the RUF (May–June 2000), the overall design features have been maintained. This section will summarize the most important operational and policy challenges at the different stages of the programme.

Disarmament

One of the most serious and intractable challenges to the disarmament stage of the programme was the failure of the combatant groups to submit the list of fighters, weaponry and their locations to peacekeepers, to allow for the planning of an effective weapon collection programme. This was a violation of an important provision of the Lomé Peace Agreement. This information would have assisted in planning the optimal location of both reception and demobilization centres. The absence of this information, coupled with the RUF's refusal to grant access to the peacekeeping forces and other key players in the programme to RUF-occupied areas, meant that the first centres were all located in government-controlled areas.

Another problem was the eligibility criteria adopted for entry into the programme, namely, the handing in of a conventional weapon. Some combatants construed this to mean a weapons buy-back programme. Consequently, some of the commanders and other senior officers attempted to disarm their junior officers in anticipation of pecuniary gain. The weapons were then given to non-combatants—wives, brothers, close relatives and friends—so they could disarm and collect benefits that could be shared with the senior officers who had initially taken these arms.

There are also the problems related to the type of weapons accepted, especially among the CDF, who are believed to have used unconventional and home-made weapons to fight the RUF/AFRC at various times during the crises. These were not accepted as eligible for the disarmament programme. Applying this policy initially caused many confrontations between the peacekeeping forces and the CDF at reception centres.

Enforcement of the weapons criteria was problematic for various other reasons, such as the arrival of combatants without weapons and former child combatants wishing to gain access to benefits meant for adult combatants. Pressure also mounted on the peacekeeping force as some of the factions, especially the ex-SLA combatants, refused to disarm to them: ex-SLA/AFRC saw ECOMOG peacekeepers as enemies with whom they had fought battles.

The absence of a clear policy and operational framework for weapons handling and destruction from the outset was also problematic. Experts who evaluated this component of the programme have criticized the peacekeeping force for poor handling and storage and the government for the absence of a policy of immediate destruction.

DEMOBILIZATION

At the demobilization stage, the most critical problem has been the refusal of disarmed ex-SLA/AFRC to demobilize for fear of losing their chances of rejoining the national army. Observers regret the absence of a military reintegration plan that would immediately screen and select for the restructured SLA. This absence led to a long period of occupation of the demobilization camp by this group of ex-combatants, taking up essential space that prevented other eligible combatants who wished to go through the civilian programme.

Another thorny problem is that of the families of ex-combatants. The camp was not initially planned to accommodate dependants. This was a mistake. Management are left with the question of what to do for a group that is critical to the lives of the ex-combatants. Most family members have been obliged to stay at the camp for prolonged periods, with implications for resource use, especially food and space.

Another challenge for demobilization has been the reluctance and/or refusal of demobilized ex-combatants to leave centres after discharge. This has been attributed to an innate fear of returning to society and lack of access to their home areas. Some ex-combatants' homes lie in areas still occupied by armed combatants.

REINTEGRATION

A key problem for social reintegration has been posed by the pattern of disarmament, which has largely been partial. Demobilized ex-combatants, especially former RUF fighters, have found it difficult to go to their homes where these are located in CDF areas. How shall enemies become reconciled and accept to live together? This is a fundamental question and must be addressed both by the government and the donor community if sustainable disarmament and constructive reintegration are to take place in Sierra Leone.

Reintegration remains the single most important aspect of the programme from the perspective of the disarmed and demobilized ex-combatant. However, major challenges remain, as full access to the whole of the country has never yet been possible. Reintegration cannot proceed if it is expected to take place in an economy destroyed by war and reduced to Freetown and two provincial capitals. The private sector is largely crippled and in need of serious investment and the public sector is starved of resources as the government's limited revenue is diverted to the war.

Against this backdrop, reintegration has been slow. Short-term job creation measures are yet to make a significant difference to the pool of unemployed non-combatant youth, both in the capital and the provincial centres.

ENVIRONMENTAL CONDITIONS

The DDR programme was conceived within a given political and security environment. A constant review of the environment is essential in order to appreciate progress or lack of progress. A few of the key issues will be highlighted in order to understand the context of the programme's current impasse.

Since the signing of the Lomé Peace Agreement, there has always been some overestimation of the RUF's good faith and political commitment. Although it was allowed to register as a political party, the RUF failed to dismantle its war machinery. Instead, it continued its incessant demands for positions in government. At one stage, it bizarrely linked disarmament to jobs for its membership.

The Lomé Peace Agreement also overlooked the fact that the AFRC, made up largely of ex-junta soldiers, was quite distinct from the RUF. Consequently, the accord never adequately addressed the needs of this group.

On the security side, there were many violations of the ceasefire by the RUF and AFRC for which no sanctions regime was ever discussed. There were verbal condemnations of these acts, but no action was taken. All factions moved troops and weapons during the ceasefire period and after signing the Lomé Peace Agreement. These movements, especially those by the RUF, were aimed at gaining territory at the expense of the government. In addition, the willingness of the Nigerian-led ECOMOG troops and UNAMSIL's determination to demonstrate robustness in peacekeeping did not match. These differences in approach among the peacekeepers were also exploited by the RUF and AFRC to provoke violations of the ceasefire and the peace agreement. Finally, the RUF challenged UNAMSIL at a demobilization centre in Makeni, northern Sierra Leone, shooting and killing four peacekeepers and abducting others. This triggered the current crises that the DDR programme and the Lomé Peace Agreement in general are undergoing.

STRATEGIES FOR THE FUTURE

Sierra Leone's DDR programme has entered a new critical phase following the recent outbreak of hostilities once again. The last two months of crisis have provided the opportunity to review past challenges. The experience gained so far will certainly make a valuable contribution to a thorough review of the programme for the next phase. A number of strategic issues should be considered in reshaping the next phase of the programme. Some of these are mentioned below.

DEADLINE FOR DISARMAMENT

One of the weaknesses in the implementation of the current programme has been the absence of a meaningful deadline. Experience has shown that, without a firmly agreed and enforceable deadline, there is always a tendency to link the DDR process to the political process, and this is a much more (time-)demanding process. The RUF has successfully exploited this to prolong or avoid the disarmament of its fighters.

Enforcement of a deadline, however, requires a much more robust posture on the part of the peacekeepers. What happens after the deadline and the possibility of an organized "cordon and search" operation for illegal weapons are critical issues. Also pertinent is the issue of recalcitrant commanders and combatants who may go against the orders of their leadership. For example, the SLA/AFRC "Okra Hills Boys," popularly known as the "West Side Junglers", have consistently defied any ultimatum pronounced for their disarmament. This may require a review of the mandate of UNAMSIL by the United Nations Security Council.

De-linking disarmament from demobilization and reintegration

The recent outbreak of hostilities by the RUF and the formation of a pro-government alliance to defend the state has resulted in the renewed proliferation of weapons and ammunition. Under the circumstances, some combatants may deliberately hide weapons with the sole aim of exploiting the current eligibility criteria for entering the DDR programme (i.e. a weapon and ammunition). As already indicated above, they may distribute weapons to civilians (non-combatants). The strategy to address this could be to offer a separate incentive for disarmament with the exclusive aim of removing all unnecessary arms from society. Entry into the demobilization and reintegration programme would then be restricted to verified combatants of the different factions.

A military reintegration plan

Before starting DDR, there needs to be a clear strategy for reintegrating interested and eligible ex-combatants into the restructured army. In Sierra Leone, there is already a Military Reintegration Plan worked out with the support of the United Kingdom government. Implementation of this plan should go alongside the civilian demobilization progamme. As combatants are disarmed, there should be an option for them to be screened for the army and selected if they satisfy the entry criteria. If they fail to satisfy those criteria, they would be required to go through the civilian programme instead. This strategy would address a number of problems that the current DDR programme faced in the last phase, including the refusal of ex-combatants to be demobilized and their long stay in encampment.

Short period of encampment or no encampment

This strategy is being implemented with the CDF, who were already residing in their home communities. When the processing of ex-combatants was speeded up in April 2000, modalities were put in place for ex-combatants who did not wish to stay in camp. However, short-period encampment was envisaged for most RUF and AFRC ex-combatants, who could not go to their homes immediately after disarmament for various reasons: for example, ex-combatants who had committed serious atrocities in home communities. In fact, there is evidence that some RUF combatants from parts of the South and East of the country have been contemplating a move to reside in the North after DDR.

PRE-DISCHARGE ORIENTATION

A pre-discharge orientation programme was part of the programme for ex-combatants at demobilization centres. However, the desire for fast-tracking, and the fact that ex-combatants never took the classes seriously, meant that this aspect of the programme has been discontinued. It will be replaced with an information session. This will provide information on DDR, especially the reintegration option, a re-entry project to help each ex-combatant into their home communities; and identify those with serious psychosocial counselling needs. This session would prepare them for other community-based programmes organized by non-governmental organizations and agencies involving non-combatants.

ASSISTANCE FOR REINSERTION

Reintegration of ex-combatants into community life is a vital part of post-conflict peace-building in Sierra Leone. It needs to be integrated into the overall strategy of the country's DDR programme. Immediately following discharge from the demobilization centres, provision had not been made for an orderly return of ex-combatants to their home communities such as is envisaged for the internally displaced and refugees. Ex-combatants who have left their home areas for a long period and/or caused problems there, like most of the RUF and AFRC ex-combatants, would need this type of assistance. This would involve more than simply transportation and the provision of a basic resettlement package.

Before the current hostilities (May–June 2000) broke out, the programme made arrangements for cash payment of US$ 300 to each ex-combatant in two instalments with a three-month interval. This would need to be revisited, with the objective of assisting with a more comprehensive in-kind reinsertion package at district level. This approach might prevent misuse of the cash and contribute to a better resettlement of the ex-combatant in the home of their choice. There are logistical implications for organizing the procurement and distribution of various items for the ex-combatants. But this inconvenience has to be weighed against the problems experienced so far and the benefits of getting ex-combatants to relocate to their home districts for social reintegration.

This leads to another very important strategic consideration that was not adequately planned for, namely, *reconciliation* at community level.

Although most Sierra Leoneans would tell you that they are ready to reconcile with erstwhile rebel combatants, the story is different when they are confronted with real ex-combatants in their communities. There are many cases of ex-combatants encountering difficulties of acceptance, even former child combatants. Most child protection agencies have complained about parents refusing to accept their own children during family tracing and reunion interventions. To address the problem of reconciliation head-on, the NCDDR should consider conducting consultative meetings at chiefdom level. These meetings should focus on the exchange of ideas about the DDR programme and the contributions the community should and could make, especially in the area of reconciliation.

REINTEGRATION STRATEGIES

Reintegration remains a key ingredient in any successful DDR process. Although this has been widely acknowledged by all the key stakeholders, this component remains hamstrung by the grinding poverty that affects all categories of the population. In Sierra Leone, poverty has deepened from over nine years of economic devastation and social dislocation. Current strategies pursued seem to be adequate, but would need to be complemented by a clear definition of the end state, namely, economic opportunities and employment for ex-combatants. Current reliance on vocational skills training and business development should be based on a clear plan derived from an assessment of appropriate needs.

Notes

[1]   On an independent analysis of this situation, see, for instance, Comfort Ero, *Sierra Leone's Security Complex*, London: Centre for Defence Studies, 2000; on security sector reform in general, see Dylan Hendrickson, *A Review of Security-Sector Reform*, London: Centre for Defence Studies, 1999.

CHAPTER 9

COMMUNITY-BASED DISARMAMENT AND POST-CONFLICT PEACE-BUILDING

Isaac Lappia

Since Sierra Leone was plunged into a brutal armed conflict in 1991, Sierra Leoneans have undergone nine years of extreme suffering inflicted by fighting forces,[1] more especially by rebel combatants. The country has been devastated by savage attacks on villages and townships. This war has been characterized by blatant human rights violations, mass killings, rape, limb amputations and torture. The conflict reached a climax when, on 6 January 1999, rebel forces stormed Freetown, the capital city, killed some 5,000 people, including women and children, and burned over 6,000 houses.

The January 1999 assault on the city and the subsequent expulsion of rebels by the Economic Community of West African States Monitoring Group (ECOMOG) revealed that there would be no imminent winner of the military conflict. The prolonged suffering of Sierra Leone's people prompted the international community to put pressure on the key players in the conflict to opt for a peaceful settlement through dialogue. This gave birth to the Lomé Accord, signed by the Revolutionary United Front (RUF) and the Government of Sierra Leone on 7 July 1999.

The Lomé Peace Accord provided a range of peace and disarmament opportunities for combatants. In some areas, local field commanders moved directly from confrontation to negotiation. For example, in the Gorama Mende (Eastern Province), Konike (Northern Province) and Nimiyama (Eastern Province) chiefdoms, the opposing forces embarked on a peace-building and disarmament programme barely five weeks after the announcement of the Lomé Accord. It should be emphasized that these local peacemakers (RUF rebels occupying the Konike chiefdom, and Kamajor militiamen of the Civil Defence Forces (CDF) in Gorama Mende and Nimiyama chiefdoms) had been fiercely fighting one another for more than five years.

Most interestingly, these community peace and disarmament initiatives were undertaken by former combatants on both sides of the conflict, without any intervention from the authorities that initially supplied them with arms.

What led the armed groups to take such early and grass-roots disarmament initiatives? The factors that gave birth to these community peace and disarmament strategies merit investigation; such is the primary aim of this paper.

FIRST STEPS TOWARD DISARMAMENT AND PEACE-BUILDING

The disarmament and peace initiatives in different parts of Sierra Leone cannot be understood unless we consider the socio-economic life of the people in the decades prior to the nine-year war. During the years of relative peace, ethnic communities lived in harmony and complemented one another, particularly in the areas of trade, social life, education and marriage. Even when the rebel war had polarized parts of the country, there is plenty of evidence that opposing forces were expressing kind sentiments concerning positive interaction with their neighbours before the war. There has been enormous expression of brotherhood and togetherness in the past. This accumulated social capital provides a strong basis for the present phase of reconciliation.

RUF Ground Commander Maruf, in his first meeting with the local CDF militiamen on 15 December 1999 in the small border town of Moyola, agreed that the lack of traditional social and economic interaction in recent years had caused much hardship and apprehension among the fighters. He had this to say:

> We are buying rice now at 500 leones for a cup. In the past our brothers from the Mendeland supplied us all kinds of food, which we bought for cheap money. Many traders have stopped selling because we are fighting the buyers, who cannot come to us. I am also depressed that for five years I could not see my second wife and daughter. They had gone to visit my in-laws, when the RUF invaded and adopted us in their absence.

This testimony lends support to the idea that many combatants have become tired of fighting and have been looking for opportunities to end hostilities with their geographical neighbours.

Hostilities on many fronts were ended through gestures of confidence—by one or other side of the fighting forces taking the initiative to end violence. Barely four months after the Lomé Accord was signed, combatants in many garrisons moved to contain the activities of their younger fighters. Numerous faction leaders wanted to express how committed they were to the maintenance of decorum in their camps by imposing greater discipline and bringing an end to unjustified acts of violence.

To demonstrate their loyalty to the Lomé Peace Agreement, the Kamajor local militia hunters released an enemy RUF rebel caught in a chiefdom border raid in the Gorama Mende chiefdom—some 9km from Masingbi, the headquarter town of the Konike chiefdom. Samuel Amos (alias Ndodoi), who was the CDF ground commander in Mondema, the Gorama Mende chiefdom headquarter town, explained:

> We one day ambushed and captured an 11-year old rebel in the chiefdom border town of Saahun. We were split on whether to execute him or not. I firmly explained that we are now under the democratic rule of law and indiscriminate killing was forbidden. The rebel was a Temne. Some of our Temne Kamajors took pity on him and pleaded that we spare his life. I ordered that he should be sent back with a strong warning letter to his commander to desist from raiding my villages. He refused to be sent back, and expressed a desire to stay with us. I firmly ordered that he take the letter to Masingbi. After three days of persuasion, he agreed to go. Joseph Wanduni, a Temne Kamajor commander was given charge of the freed captive, and ordered to ensure his safe delivery to the rebel commanders in Masingbi. Commander Maruf quickly joyfully wrote to me in Mondema, thanking me for the brotherly way I treated his fighter and requested that I organize a preliminary meeting between them and all the Temne Kamajors in my camp. We have, after that meeting, been constantly meeting to strengthen the new peace we have built ourselves.

Masingbi and Mondema lie more than 50km to the north of Saahun, in the centre of Sierra Leone—this shows the large areas covered by the different guerrilla groups and the way in which communications can, however, move swiftly between regions.

This story goes on to reveal how the warring parties, in their meetings, could not discover any reasonable, just cause for rising up in arms against one another. The general feeling among the rebel ranks was that they had been manipulated and wrongly used. Many rebels, it was discovered, had been forcibly conscripted to fight for "good pay" that was promised at the end of the victorious rebellion.

As the levels of interaction and confidence rose, the combatants continued to engage in activities that could help them rediscover the common development vision they shared prior to the nine years of bloody conflict. On 25 December 1999, a football match was played between Masingbi and Mondema and this was followed by a night disco. Fighters took turns to expiate openly the destructive nature of the war and pledged their commitments to developing lasting peace in their region. More than a dozen former RUF combatants stayed with the Kamajors for close to a week after the Christmas celebrations before returning to Masingbi.

The level of confidence between the two sides continued to increase. Trade links gradually opened up, and foreign goods appeared for the first time in the Mondema, Jaiama Sewafe and Punduru markets.

HOW PEOPLE ARE DISARMING

All the rank and file on all sides of the Sierra Leone crisis feel the weight of the power of arms. Arms provide "power" and remain the prime means of survival for most combatants. These weapons are the principal factor for the prolongation of conflict. Inadequate supply of arms and ammunition mitigates conflicts. Poorly equipped combatants are soon demotivated and become less imbued with the Maoist notion that "power grows from the barrel of the gun". Poorly equipped fighters can more easily be persuaded to stop making war.

The question of arms is critical in any disarmament and peace-building process. The rebels, in their initial meeting with the CDF militiamen in Masingbi, discussed the active role of arms in conflicts. A senior RUF commander, Savage Sesay (alias Ambush Tech), had this to say:

> We will not succeed in our confidence-building drive with all these guns in the hand of especially these children. A single incident in the process

may again spark off violence and frustrate our efforts. As for me, I am no more interested in fighting, I am committed to the peace accord. Whoever had been my follower must be ready to lay down his gun. I am therefore proposing that we disarm all the under aged fighters and keep their weapons for the DDR.

The commander's proposal to disarm the youngest fighters was unanimously supported by their former antagonists on the government side. After the meeting, the commanders in both camps set out to collect all arms and ammunition from fighters under 16 years of age, together with adults whose hands were "light with guns". It was agreed that adults who had questionable emotional maturity could not be trusted to handle guns.

In Masingbi, RUF Commander Maruf had all the collected stocks of weapons packed at the RUF headquarters office, in the "Strong Room", where war captives had been held. Surplus weapons kept by adults were also collected and stowed away. Lack of absolute trust on both sides, however, encouraged some adult combatants to continue to carry weapons. The general agreement was that the weapons collected must be immediately handed to the DDR team on its first visit to Masingbi.

In the Gorama Mende and Nimiyama chiefdoms, the chiefs approached the disarmament process in a more organized way. In the context of the general disarmament programme enshrined in the Lomé Accord and upheld by their former antagonists, the chiefs proposed to hold a consultative meeting of elders in the two chiefdoms. In this consultative forum, it was discovered that other factors unrelated to the peace accord stimulated the bush disarmament process.

According to Mr Musa Bah, a powerful section chief in Mondema, the disarmament process was accelerated by the many cases of fatal shooting incidents in the chiefdoms, leading to serious condemnation by civil groups of the ill-disciplined fighting forces. The combatants also resorted to harassment and extortion of money from civilians, which occasionally caused serious confrontations. To address the numerous human rights violations and to promote the Lomé peace initiative, chiefdom elders met in November 1999 to work out plans for disarming combatants before the DDR team even reached the chiefdoms. Child combatants were selected to be the first to disarm.

Initially, the disarmament proposals met with some criticism from the fighting youths. They argued that nobody had the right to remove the guns from their possession. They claimed that, since they had acquired their guns from their enemies in battle, nobody had ever given them weapons: therefore nobody should have the right to remove them. Notwithstanding this initial problem, the chiefs' proposal for disarmament went well. Before the subsequent general meeting with the RUF even took place, the chiefs disarmed many child combatants. For the adult combatants to disarm, some incentive was needed. The chiefs explained that only combatants who had surrendered their weapons in advance would be recommended to the DDR team for compensation. Meanwhile, those who refused to disarm voluntarily would be forced to hand over their weapons and would lose all benefits.

Many adult combatants feared losing out, and therefore handed in their weapons. The use of weapons thereafter was considerably suppressed. Those adult fighters who retained their weapons took the greatest care not to expose them. As these initial disarmament exercises continued, both parties strongly resolved that no arms should be carried to any of the subsequent peace-building meetings between the opposing forces.

Any infringement of this disarmament law by the local militiamen was met with a stringent response from the rebel forces. At a subsequent general meeting, seven Kamajors entered, well armed with light machine-guns, much to the surprise of the rebel commanders. They were subsequently reproached for breaking the law and were asked to surrender their guns to the meeting guards outside. The Kamajors expected to get their weapons back after the meeting, but the seven guns were never returned. The Kamajors refrained from pushing too hard for the return of their weapons for two reasons: firstly, they were in the enemy zone; and secondly, they recognized that they had gone against the law to which they were a party. The confiscation of these weapons was a punishment for violation of the law and a stern warning that all parties should give peace a chance.

It was judged from the fighters' reactions that they had reaffirmed their belief in peace-building because the objective of their armed struggle was not clear. Often and again unclear motives for continuing the war have generated an increasingly conscious desire for peace in the fighters. Those who want to see a peaceful settlement to the fighting are in conflict with the hardliners. The new desire within the fighting forces to begin peace-building has created an uncomfortable gap between those in the bush and the politically motivated warlords who reap the benefits from their struggle. In some cases, loyalty has waned and splits have emerged in combatant camps. The statement of RUF town commander Komeh (alias "Specialist", as he was considered the expert in using rocket-propelled grenades) supports this assertion:

> Up to now, I have not been adequately told of what I am fighting for. They say we will get pay at the end of the war—but we are many. Some say if we get power, we will get posts in the government and the army—but I don't want to work for government. I want to get pay but how are we going to be paid?

The fuzzy nature of what profit they will actually gain in the end worries many RUF fighters. The fighters are beginning to wonder what concrete benefits they will receive in exchange for all the pains of the war, and through what mechanism such benefit may eventually reach them. The confusion surrounding their situation has persuaded some to leave the rebel forces. They have started to realize that gifted and bloodthirsty warlords have created a pool of delusion in which they have destroyed their own society. Many combatants are now looking for every possible avenue that may lead to the road of peace.

RECOMMENDATIONS

The great sense of identity in Sierra Leone communities should assist them to achieve reconciliation after a decade of violence. It should be possible to replicate the successful peacemaking initiatives we have described in other villages, irrespective of their ethnic mix. It is true that the war has dangerously polarized communities whose different ethnic components used to be interdependent and inseparable. The conflict in Sierra Leone has been especially damaging because of the atrocities carried out by rebel, occupying forces. Through indiscriminate use of drugs on children, RUF commanders caused these young fighters to carry out horrendous acts of abuse in their native communities, sometimes even against their own families. These actions have poisoned the minds of social groups and set them against one another.

However, in the face of continued difficulties and occasional armed confrontation, we remain confident that the capacity of the Sierra Leonean society to build consensus and to create communal reconciliation remains strong.

Many communities may want to open up to those against whom they had struggled in arms; but they may lack the confidence to do so, because of the terrible actions they have witnessed. The following ideas offer new ways in which peace-building, confidence-building and local disarmament can be encouraged.

1. Arrange for community heads and war commanders to meet together in an atmosphere of friendliness. This activity could engender confidence in all parties, and could reinforce the message of "no more war".

2. Encourage community leaders to work out among themselves modalities for disarming civilian groups, and especially young fighters. It is vitally important to drive home the message that easy access to supplies of arms and ammunition could undermine the new and fragile peace-building process. It is therefore an urgent priority to collect and destroy, *openly and publicly,* all weapons and ammunition as quickly as possible.

3. Arrange a general meeting between the opposing forces in an atmosphere of festivity, and give combatants adequate opportunities to expiate their actions and reaffirm their commitment to peace.

4. Enable the flow of combatants across borders/territories, so they can visit each other. This flow of combatants should strengthen confidence and could mitigate—if not eradicate—further preparations for war. People from other communities could be encouraged to monitor the evolution of events in opposite camps.

5. Organize a disarmament, demobilization and reintegration (DDR) sensitization programme for all the combatants, to increase their understanding of the Lomé Peace Accord. This could strengthen their motivation for peace.

6. Speedily put in place local, democratic structures of governance to enhance the transfer of power from combatants to official structures obeying the rule of law. Civil rule should facilitate the disarmament process and decrease the levels of violence.

7. Provide attractive conditions for combatants in the demobilization camps, which may lure reluctant combatants into disarming and joining the DDR process. Experience in the DDR camps during 1998 showed that the absence of favourable conditions actually discouraged combatants from surrendering their arms. Journalists reported in late 1998 that poor camp food, lack of entertainment or useful occupations and the total absence of any training for future employment or any other form of preparation for civilian life were factors which led ex-combatants in Lungi camp to advise their friends in the bush to hold on to their guns and not to join the DDR process.

Notes

1   The various armed forces in Sierra Leone include the Revolutionary United Front (RUF); the old Sierra Leone Army (SLA), which joined with the RUF in 1997 and formed the Armed Forces Revolutionary Council (AFRC); the Civil Defence Forces (CDF), of which the Kamajors are mainly the Mende component; the ECOMOG force; the UN military observers of UNOMSIL and peacekeepers of UNAMSIL; British marines and training units; and finally, the new Sierra Leone Defence Force, which was formed in 1999 under a Nigerian commander and which is participating in security matters, although it is not yet properly structured or trained. The Sierra Leone Police Force is in charge of enforcing law and order.

CHAPTER 10

WOMEN AGAINST WEAPONS:
A LEADING ROLE FOR WOMEN IN DISARMAMENT

Binta Mansaray

> Blama Camp—Sierra Leone. One 25-year-old woman said that she had delivered a still-born baby the day before rebels of the Revolutionary United Front attacked her village in 1998. She was unable to flee with most of the other villagers, and five rebels took turn raping her, she said. When her husband tried to intervene, they killed him. "I thought at first I was dealing with human beings, so I was sad and confused because I had just delivered a dead baby; I was bloody and weak", she said between two sobs. "But they were not human beings. After they left I gave up, and I wanted to die. I had no reason to live any more."
>
> **Doug Farah**, "A War Against Women".[1]

WOMEN AND POLITICS IN SIERRA LEONE:
TOOLS AND VICTIMS

The ongoing armed conflict in Sierra Leone did not happen by accident. It was generated by more than two decades of bad governance that led to the corruption and, finally, the total collapse of the Sierra Leonean state. The violent conflict swept the nation into a gigantic whirlwind of horror. In this process of cumulative decay, women were used as instruments of corruption, and corruption was used as a weapon against women.

Following independence in 1961, Sierra Leone enjoyed a brief period of good governance under Sir Milton Margai. This period is still remembered as a "golden era". In 1964, Sir Milton died and was succeeded by his brother Albert Margai. Albert Margai's rule was characterized by large-scale corruption, which his successor Siaka Stevens took to horrific proportions, ultimately destroying the integrity of all state institutions.

In addition to being highly corrupt, Siaka Stevens's regime was overwhelmingly male dominated. Over ninety per cent of his cabinet ministers and parliamentarians were men. In his 1982 government there were no women at all. Throughout Stevens's era women never held more than two cabinet positions at any given term of office. This pattern remained true for all the succeeding regimes (mostly led by army officers) up to the present time. It was Sierra Leone's male-dominated political apparatus that caused the collapse of the state. Some of its most disastrous decisions included the abolition of political parties and local government. Governance was removed from the people. The checks and balances needed for accountability, as well as transparency, were undermined.

Women, the disadvantaged, other half of society, bore the brunt of the above-mentioned, essentially male-framed and male-oriented, decisions. In addition, women were specifically targeted for political manipulation and exploitation: often, semi-literate and illiterate women who were ignorant of good governance but who had influence in their communities. In these categories were the Hajas.[2] The politicians also targeted non-Muslim female religious leaders to garner grass-roots support for the governing All People's Congress (APC). Influential traditional women were also identified to mobilize the grass roots, such as the wives or female relatives of chiefs. The "recruiting" was as simple as it was machiavellian: toward the election campaign, politicians would contact identified women and offer them rice quotas through the "PL480 system".[3] Contrary to its intended purpose, the rice aid was used to woo the Hajas, church leaders and traditional women leaders to galvanize and mobilize women to vote for the politicians and sing their praises. The tragic irony (for women) was that these female folk were all too happy to be "recognized" by high-level politicians, whom they referred to as "Big Men". They did not appreciate the politics of gender exploitation to which they were being subjected. They did not realize that their lives were governed by unjust customary laws, condemning them to the status objects for their entire life on earth.

As a consequence, these women sang and danced: but not in return for better conditions of living, nor for community development programmes, nor for the establishment of well-equipped health centres, nor the socio-economic opportunities that they badly needed. They sang and danced for a pittance, a few cups of rice and a bunch of promises that were never fulfilled. After elections, when the clocks swang back to "politics as usual", women were marginalized as usual. And there they would stay, ignored by the real power brokers until the next election campaign, when Big Men would again come, offering attention, "consideration", a couple of cups of rice and a new bunch of empty promises.[4] The energies that grass-roots women expended in dancing and singing could have been used in a wiser, more productive way.

As far as issues of post-conflict peace-building, disarmament and arms regulation are concerned, the role of these women is crucial. Most of these marginalized singing and dancing women are mothers of marginalized youths: children who failed at school or who never had the opportunity to go to school. Those very same children became street children in peacetime and soldiers in wartime. Hundreds of others were victims: killed, or gang-raped, or mutilated. We now know for certain that youth drop-outs neglected by the APC government were the first "elements" recruited by a movement that came to be known as the Revolutionary United Front (RUF), one of the most atrocious and deadly armed movements of the twentieth century.

WOMEN AFFECTED BY WAR

Their institutionalization of corruption blinded politicians in Sierra Leone to the needs of the masses in general, and those of women in particular. A huge political, economic, social and psychological gap developed between the leaders and the people. This "fatal gap" created the opportunity for the emergence, in March 1991, of the RUF. It is interesting to note that the male-dominated politics of the government apparatus was reproduced by the guerrilla movement. The founding leaders of the RUF, Foday Sankoh, Abu Kanu and Rashid Mansaray, were all men. Initially the RUF declared it would "save" the nation from the corrupt APC government. However, no sooner did the movement start in 1991 than it turned into a movement against the people of Sierra Leone in general and women and children in particular.

The "revolution" of the Revolutionary United Front represented in no respect redemption for women. On the contrary, the RUF committed unspeakable crimes. It invented a new form of "war": cutting off noses, ears, legs and plucking out eyes. RUF combatants also sexually mutilated civilians, raped and gang-raped women and girls, ordered sons and fathers to rape their mothers and daughters—upon penalty of their own death if they refused. The RUF abducted women and children, whom they forcibly conscripted as sex slaves or as combatants—small arms and light weapons can easily be operated by children and women.

And the worst was yet to come. The launch of the RUF movement in 1991 was only the beginning in a series of political tragedies.

- In April 1992, the APC government of President Momoh was toppled by young officers and a National Provisional Ruling Council (NPRC) was formed.
- In May 1997, the democratically elected government of Ahmad Tejan Kabbah was ousted by another group of young officers and an Armed Forces Revolutionary Council (AFRC) was formed.
- In January 1999 Freetown, the capital city, was invaded jointly by the RUF and the AFRC.

This endless, escalating violence had a devastating physical and psychological impact on women and their children. One of the very first consequences of war was that women were uprooted from home and community and became refugees or internally displaced persons. It is estimated that two thirds of Sierra Leone's population were displaced within the country or became refugees in neighbouring countries. Of these two thirds, about seventy five per cent were women and children. The destruction of homes and social services, combined with forced displacement of a large number of the population, has placed women in a very dangerous and precarious situation. Women in areas controlled by rebels continue to suffer and die from malnutrition, starvation and preventable and curable diseases. Unwanted pregnancies and the spread of sexually transmitted diseases—particularly HIV/AIDS—during this crisis are a matter of grave concern to society at large and women in particular. This is not a surprise, since one of the most favoured "war strategies" in the orgy of violence has been that of subjecting women to sexual abuse and exploitation. Women and girls have experienced the most dehumanizing rape and sexual violence during hostilities. Many have been carried off;

stories from the abducted who managed to escape give accounts of women and girls dying on a daily basis as a result of gang rape and sexual mutilation. Women have been subjected to the most horrendous physical, sexual and psychological violation.

This is specifically a gender question in Sierra Leone's armed struggle for power. It is a sadistic and systematic victimization of women by senseless—and sometimes aimless—fighters.

The psychological trauma of war-affected women is one of the most complicated long-term consequences that Sierra Leone, as a nation, will have to face in the post-war reconstruction process. Whether they were abducted, raped or gang-raped, sexually enslaved, forced into combat, witnessed their children become "child soldiers", or were amputated or maimed, these war-affected women will need specific treatment within ongoing post-war reconstruction programmes. The country must be rebuilt from shattered lives and broken dreams. For some women, life will never be the same; while men can move on, remarry and start new families, female victims of rape have no such chance. Although they are victims, their lives are forever marred by the social stigma associated with rape.

The socio-economic effects of the war on women are enormous and depressing. In the aftermath of the war, the socio-economic status of women has changed. There are more female heads of households, more single parents and thousands of war widows. This has created extreme economic, social and psychological hardship, with destitute women left alone to care for children and extended family members. Economic activities that women engaged in, such as petty trading, soap-making, tie-dying and farming, were all destroyed during hostilities. Despite their resilience, many women will find it hard to survive and prosper in the post-war economy.

THE ROLE OF WOMEN IN ARMED CONFLICT

Having been the main victims of wanton violence, Sierra Leone's women are well placed to know the true price of peace. For that reason, they can play a determinant role in post-war peace-building. Women are certainly the best hope for sustainable peace in Sierra Leone today.

We should, however, avoid the caricature of "naturally peace-loving" women. Trite expressions like "women love peace and men make war" are misleading. Real-life situations in Sierra Leone show that all is a question of circumstances. Women represent the best bet for peace, not because they are "naturally" or "inherently" peace-loving human beings—as compared to "naturally or inherently war-loving males"—but because women are usually excluded from the male-dominated political groups which take warlike decisions. When talking about the role of women in peace-building, we should objectively face the reality that, in violent situations, women can be as ferocious as men. A couple of instances from the Sierra Leonean war will illustrate the point.

WOMEN AS AGGRESSORS

Records of the male-dominated armed confrontation in Sierra Leone show that although essentially victims, women sometimes became protagonists. The hidden truth is that, in many instances, women played a significant, "active" role in violence. And it is important to note that the easy use of small arms and light weapons facilitated women's role as aggressors. Small arms require very little training.

Women became involved, as offending actors, in the conflict for a variety of reasons.

- Some women voluntarily joined the movement: sometimes to escape from daily life as second-class citizens and to demonstrate in a violent way that they were capable of doing whatever men could do. Perhaps this was a bid for gender equality. Being marginalized by both customary practice and the APC regime, women's involvement in armed conflict can be seen as a revolt. They wanted to identify with a movement that they thought would liberate them and fulfil their fundamental human need for recognition. The protection of human dignity is what they have been yearning for.
- Some of those who were abducted, according to testimonies of some aggressors, subsequently chose to stay in the movement. They were trained as combatants. Hopeful that the RUF would take control of the country's resources, these women believed that they would enjoy their rights to education, health and freedom as promised by the rebel leader Foday Sankoh.

- Other women became perpetrators of violence because they were trapped in the movement and just could not get out. Women involved in the AFRC soldiers' movement were also disgruntled with life in the military, one of the casualties of state corruption.

According to one former member of the RUF war council, women were also members of the war council, although they were outnumbered by men.[5] In the 1992–1994 war council, out of twenty one members, five were women. Susan Lahai, currently Deputy Minister of Transport, was appointed overall commander of the combat medical unit. The late Memuna Sesay, who died in combat, was appointed overall commander of female combatants. Mama Combey and Mamei Abu were also members of the war council. Winifred Palmer became a training commandant. The former RUF member declared that the women were happy to be members of the war council because of the social recognition that came with it.

From the testimony of female victims of violence, these women aggressors were sometimes the most vicious. Sia Lebbie of Jaiama Sewafe in Kono remembers how she was threatened with death by a female RUF: "The woman ... was with the other rebels in combat when they came to my house. The man tried to rape me and I didn't want him to do that to me, then the rebel woman told me if I refused to be raped she will kill me so I just obeyed because I didn't want to die."[6]

Women who took part in fighting generated headlines like, "Woman Commando Terrorizes Kono Highway". This was a story of a female rebel commando captured by government forces. The article says: "At the Government hospital yesterday in Makeni laid the corpses of five persons who fell in a rebel ambush 8:30 am ... The attack at five-mile on the Makeni–Kono highway was said to have been spearheaded by a woman rebel commando ... who used bayonet, gun and matches and kerosene to burn the victims."[7]

There are also testimonies by the civil militias—the Kamajors—about their encounters with women fighters. According to an interview with the Kamajors, "we have in the past been fighting against female combatants and they are heavily armed". Women committed looting using violence or the threat of violence. One case concerned Auntie Rhoda in Makeni in November 1998, whose son was killed while she herself was held at gunpoint by a female commando who stole all her jewellery and valuables.

Looting was also a reason why some women stayed in the movement: in a society which had so deprived them, they knew that they would never get the opportunity legally to earn a fraction of their gain from raiding and looting towns and villages.

Women aggressors also committed rape. According to data from Victims of Sexual Abuse, 11.75 per cent of a total of 2,110 rape cases reported were committed by female perpetrators (see Table 1).

Table 1: Data of victims of sexual abuse by RUF/AFRC forces, collected between March 1999 and January 2000[8]

Age (Years)	Male	Female	Total
0–5	31	68	**99**
6–12	142	157	**299**
13–18	63	628	**691**
19–25	7	852	**859**
Over 27	5	157	**162**
Total	**248**	**1,862**	**2,110**

Women carried out amputations: there was an RUF fighter called "Adama Cut Hand". According to the testimony of a rape victim in Magoma, her husband was amputated by "Adama Cut Hand" when their village was attacked in August 1998. She still does not know the whereabouts of her husband after she fled for her life.

A handful of AFRC women (renegade women soldiers and those who collaborated with them) were charged and convicted of treason. For instance, Major Kula Samba was the fifteenth accused at the treason trial that followed the reinstatement of President Tejan Kabbah. She was believed to have been a member of the AFRC war council. "She took the oath of office as AFRC Secretary of State, Social Welfare, Children and Gender Affairs. An active member of the junta who travelled abroad to seek recognition and raise funds for the AFRC."[9] She was charged on seven counts of Treason, Mutiny, Failure to suppress mutiny, Treason (endeavouring), Treason (soliciting), Treason (Aiding and Abetting) and

Conspiracy. She was tried and convicted on all counts but Failure to suppress mutiny. Kula Samba was sentenced to death and executed in October 1998.

The high-profile 75-year-old Nancy Steele, an APC stalwart, was convicted of treason and sentenced to ten years in prison for taking up an appointment as director of the Sierra Leone Shipping Agency under the AFRC junta. She died in a stampede when the rebels broke into the Pademba Road prison to release all prisoners during the 6 January 1999 invasion of Freetown.

Kainde Bangura was the eleventh accused at the 1998 treason trials. She was convicted of treason and sentenced to ten years in prison. Mayilla Yansaneh, twelfth accused, was convicted of treason and sentenced to death. Matilda King, third accused and convicted of treason, was sentenced to death. Bangura, Yansaneh and King were not executed. The rebels set them free in January 1999 and they eventually benefited from the blanket amnesty provided by the Lomé Peace Accord.

WOMEN AS COLLABORATORS

There were also female "collaborators". These are women who were not at the war front, but who incited and supported the combatants. Into this category fall spouses and female relatives of combatants: those of the RUF and AFRC on the one hand and of pro-government forces like the civil militias and the Economic Community of West African States Monitoring Group (ECOMOG) on the other.

Pro-rebel women acted as spies by dating pro-government forces or infiltrating their headquarters and leaking relevant information to the rebels. One of the most notorious cases is that of Kuku Sheriff, who at times made headlines like "Kuku: still living it up in Freetown". The story went: "*Concord Times* set eyes on the gorgeous Mandingo mid-forties lady at the Wilberforce Barracks ECOMOG headquarters ... she was waiting to see Brig. Gen. Maxwell Khobe.... Perhaps the Intelligence Unit is not aware it could be a security risk to let her freely not only in society but right into the security web of the Peacekeepers. Reports say she is also often seen around the other military quarters in Freetown ... She is infiltrating the network, unknown to the ECOMOG security apparatus."[10]

Women smuggled small arms and light weapons by carrying them among the goods they carried on their backs, heads or in suitcases. Smuggling was made easier by the fact that small arms and light weapons are easy to hide and to carry. According to the testimony of a member of the Civil Defence Unit, Saladeen Fuad, who was manning checkpoints at different locations during the armed conflict, a woman was caught carrying a weapon in a black plastic bag in which she had her underwear. Mr Fuad also testified that a woman at the Kissy Texaco checkpoint in the East End of Freetown had placed a weapon on her back and carried her child on top of the weapon she was carrying: "When the rebels were infiltrating Freetown every day, we were searching everyone at the checkpoints. This woman's child was crying bitterly, so I told her to take her child off her back to pacify him. She refused. I insisted and took the child off her back, then a pistol fell off her back. I detained her, she kept telling me that she was not aware of the weapon."[11] Another woman was caught carrying a weapon in the basket of fresh fish she was selling, apparently trying to smuggle it.

Newspapers also covered these real-life testimonies. *Concord Times* carried the headline "Ferry Junction Drama: Haja uses Poda Poda to smuggle arms". According to the newspaper, a "prominent business woman Haja Ramatulai was picked up by ECOMOG personnel at Kissy Ferry Junction Sunday while attempting to smuggle arms and ammunition through the security post … Her arrest has fuelled speculation that there are junta elements inside Freetown collaborating with those in the forest. She was in a Poda Poda with a suitcase in which she had hidden a grenade and pistol."[12]

Pro-rebel women collaborators also helped the rebels to infiltrate communities and use civilians as human shields. This made it harder for pro-government forces, who fought conventional warfare, to identify and destroy rebels. Women provided the rebels with food and shelter while the latter waited for the opportune time to strike, and they also identified anti-rebel neighbours who became specific targets of rebels. On the other hand, pro-government women identified rebel collaborators, and this at times resulted in the lynching and extra-judicial killing of alleged collaborators by pro-government forces—ECOMOG and the civil militias. Some acted as spies and encouraged pro-government forces to annihilate the rebels. They provided food and shelter for ECOMOG and the civil militias.

As these examples show, if this was not a women's war, objectivity demands that we recognize that some women—a tiny minority—sometimes played an important role in the conduct of hostilities. The most important historical fact remains, however, that while these "warring women" resorted to arms or revolt against the system, other women—an overwhelming majority—were trying to change the course of events by advocating democracy and peace.

WOMEN AND PEACEMAKING IN SIERRA LEONE

The devastating war seemed like it would go on forever. Sierra Leonean women were the first to experience war fatigue. They became sick and tired of losing their husbands to the war, having their children abducted, living in perpetual fear and seeing the breakdown of the family units and communities that meant so much to them. Something had to be done: that was the collective and natural feeling of the majority of women.

The women's movement became vibrant from 1994 onwards with pioneers like Zainab Bangura, Amy Smythe, Elizabeth Lavalie and Dr Kadi Sesay (to name a few) taking the lead in mobilizing and galvanizing civil society to call for peace, democracy and a cessation of hostilities. Civil society (and especially women's associations) had been marginalized by centralized government and by war. Now civil society and women's associations manifested their ideas and ideals through workshops, seminars and conferences.

The message of these pioneering women was peace and democracy. Democratic governance could provide outlets for expressing grievances, and the checks and balances needed to curb corruption and generate a system that is not oppressive. Noting that women had used weapons to revolt against corruption, civil society organizations sought to identify the causes of violence and to find remedies to the escalating war. Women had the feeling—and offered facts as proof—that structural violence was the hallmark of the male hegemony over Sierra Leone since independence. From Albert Margai to Siaka Stevens, from Stevens to Joseph Momoh, from Momoh to Valentine Strasser, from Strasser to Julius Maada Bio, all the supreme leaders have been male, and many have been military. These women proposed to reform those institutions of the state that embody covert violence—which has come to be called "structural violence".[13] The eradication of systemic violence is one challenge women have undertaken in launching a campaign for democracy and peace.

In 1994, Dr Kadi Sesay, in her capacity as chair of the National Commission for Democracy and Human Rights (NCDHR), held seminars and used the media (radio and TV) for civic education, democracy and human rights sensitization campaigns. Her democracy programme contributed to preparing the electorate for nationwide participatory electoral democracy, which bore fruit in the massive turnout for the 1996 democratic elections. Meanwhile, Florence Dillsworth became chair of Freetown City Council, and was a very dynamic advocate for good governance. In a two-day workshop held at the British Council on 8 March 1994, she declared her unflinching determination that women shall beat all odds in their struggle for peace and democracy: "Women have been suppressed, abused, ill-used, misused and marginalized, but we are a breed that is difficult to kill."[14] She demonstrated the conviction of her statement throughout her tenure by relentlessly advocating the resuscitation of local government, which was one of the casualties of Siaka Stevens's centralized corruption. Florence Dillsworth called for more decentralization, and for women's representation and participation in local government, which are essential components of democracy and stability. She advocated women's rights and made recommendations for the creation of gender units in government institutions to encourage the participation of women in promoting peace. Dr Kadi Sesay and Ms Florence Dillsworth tirelessly committed their institutions to promoting the movement for peace and democracy. They encouraged women to join the political processes of the country. In this way women would feel involved rather than marginalized.

In 1995, a great mobilization for peace began. Mrs Elizabeth Lavalie resigned her position as Bank Manageress at the National Development Bank, and on 24 January 1995 she led a demonstration for peace organized by the Eastern Region Women's Movement for Peace. In Bo, Sierra Leone's second city, Southern Province organized a similar demonstration in the course of the same year.

In February 1995 Dr Fatmata Boie Kamara, a paediatrician, led a March for Peace organized by the Women's Movement for Peace, to express concern for women's plight in the war and to call for conflict resolution at the negotiating table and through peace education. In March 1995 the Women's Movement for Peace held a press conference. They read out a letter they had sent to the rebel leader Foday Sankoh, calling for a stop to the madness and senseless bloodshed. At the press conference, Dr Boie Kamara and the Public Relations Officer for the Women's Movement for Peace, Isha Dyfan, made the stance of women very clear. Isha Dyfan said: "Women have a specific role in conflict resolution and our common concern here is to bring the war to a speedy end with independence and neutrality being our main focus."[15] Dr Boie Kamara added: "Since the public is in full support of a peaceful resolution of the conflict, we are going to keep harping on this until the warring factions come to the negotiating table".[16]

However, in January 1996 a palace coup took place. The chairman of the NPRC, Valentine Strasser, was ousted and Julius Maada Bio became president. It soon became apparent that Maada Bio wanted to circumvent the elections, scheduled for 26 February 1996 as agreed by the 17 August 1995 National Consultative Conference (NCC, now known as "Bintumani 1"). Maada Bio made a tour of the country to lobby and "advise" traditional leaders to speak out against holding elections, in order to reverse the consensus of the NCC. After his nationwide tour, Maada Bio informed Sierra Leoneans that, according to what he had heard, the people did not want elections until peace was achieved.

Among civil society organizations, women again took a lead in arguing that elections should go hand in hand with peace negotiations. An election is an event, they argued, whereas peace is an ongoing process. Maada Bio proposed convening a second Consultative Conference, confident that traditional leaders would influence members of their constituencies to vote overwhelmingly against having elections before peace. Thus "Bintumani 2" was convened. Civil society leaders—notably Zainab Bangura, Amy Smythe, Isha Dyfan and Yasmin Jusu-Sheriff as members of the Women's Forum—launched a sensitization campaign, holding rallies, conferences and meetings to get enough people to vote in favour of holding elections. They wrote position papers and issued press releases unequivocally reaffirming their commitment to elections. The power of the civil society campaign was great enough that, on 12 February, the scheduled day for the Bintumani 2 conference, the military junta attempted to sabotage the conference, barricading the streets and highways to make it impossible for participants to turn out in large numbers. But the women could not be deterred. They found short cuts; some were threatened and beaten, but they still made it to the conference centre. They were united in their struggle in action and in words.

Here is the statement read by all women delegates at Bintumani 2: "We support that peace negotiations and elections must go hand in hand as previously agreed. We therefore demand that the elections ... go ahead on 26 February 1996 as agreed at the national consultative conference and approved by the NPRC government, the political parties, civil society and the Interim National Electoral Commission."[17] Women also made a statement to the head of state to reaffirm their stance on holding democratic elections: "We believe that successful elections on 26 February 1996 ... will be the basis for all to build a better Sierra Leone."[18]

Mrs Shirley Gbujama, who chaired both Bintumani 1 and 2 conferences, complemented the women's effort and played a crucial role by steering the consultations toward a positive outcome for democratic elections. She made sure that no one manipulated the process. For instance, a self-proclaimed spokesman for the paramount chiefs (who was not a chief, but a pro-junta stooge) wanted to declare on behalf of the chiefs against holding elections. The chair did not allow him to speak on the grounds that since he was not himself a chief, he did not have the moral authority to talk on behalf of chiefs. Mrs Gbujama knew that the paramount chiefs would be embarrassed to be associated with a public stance; but she obliged them to appoint a paramount chief as their spokesman. A paramount chief spokesman was appointed, who grudgingly declared a pro-election position. This was crucial, given the influence of traditional leaders. As their next ploy, pro-junta activists tried to stage a commotion outside the conference hall, then attempted to persuade Mrs Gbujama to discontinue the conference for security reasons. She refused to be manipulated, and used her discretion to continue while asking that the commotion be investigated.

Women's efforts were recognized also in the fact that the chair of the NCDHR, Dr Kadi Sesay, made the opening statement to both conferences. Being an opinion leader and a household name because of her democracy civic education campaign on the radio and on television, her voice was respected by both men and women. This also helped to influence a positive outcome for elections.

The Bintumani conferences (1 and 2) significantly contributed to the high turnout for the 1996 presidential elections. Women participated as observers, presiding officers and advocates. Even when the military junta opened fire to intimidate the electorate on election day, women ensured that elections took place by moving from one polling station to another to encourage the electorate not to be intimidated, but to stay in the polling booths until had they cast their votes.

Women's active participation did not stop at the end of the accomplishment of electoral democracy. More women's organizations were established. More women were chosen to head organizations. Women in Action, Women in Need, the Campaign for Good Governance, Women Accord 97, Women in Crisis, Women in the Media and Sisters United are all examples of organizations which gave women a high profile in civil society.

When the democratically elected government of Ahmad Tejan Kabbah was overthrown on 25 May 1997, women played a significant role in ensuring that the military regime that was formed—the Armed Forces Revolutionary Council (AFRC)—was not recognized. Civil society organized civil disobedience—everyone refused to go to work; banks, businesses and civil service machinery came to a halt. The civil disobedience was a spontaneous reaction of civil society, saying "No" to coups and counter-coups, which could be a deterrent to future coup plotters. Women played a crucial role in sustaining the momentum of the civil disobedience. This was in large part a result of the political awareness sensitization campaign run by women. The late first lady, Mrs Patricia Kabbah, relentlessly appealed to the citizens of Sierra Leone and to women in particular not to give up their struggle for democracy. To carry out her appeal she launched a sensitization campaign through the FM 98.1 Radio Democracy, which was established on 7 July 1997 to counter AFRC propaganda. Mrs Kabbah made trips to America and Belgium to seek support for the restoration of democracy. While in exile in Guinea, Mrs Kabbah tried to get scholarships for students in exile so that they would not become drop-outs, and she also encouraged the Forum for African Women Educationalists (FAWE) in Guinea, which was working to curb the staggering illiteracy rate of women and girls in the subregion. This was to inspire women to keep hope alive in their struggle for democracy to prevail.

Mrs Zainab Bangura went into exile in neighbouring Guinea. While in exile she organized demonstrations and mobilized civil society. Bangura set up an office on behalf of the Campaign for Good Governance (CGG), which served as a venue for all civil society organizations. They could meet, design their various strategies to defy the military junta, and call for the restoration of democracy. CGG served as a forum for information- and experience-sharing and collaboration among civil society groups, so that they could speak with one voice to achieve one goal—the restoration of democracy. Zainab Bangura ensured that civil society in exile was in constant touch with those who stayed home through Radio Democracy. Women in exile participated in the struggle. Disguising their voices and using pseudonyms so that the junta would not persecute their relatives in Sierra Leone, they sent anti-junta messages to the people.

Women also formed a movement called the Women's National Salvation Front. Anti-junta discussions were recorded and aired on Radio Democracy. The women in Freetown countered the propaganda of the AFRC by exposing its misdeeds. The women in Freetown were not able to organize as a group, but some of them acted as undercover agents. They infiltrated the junta. Crucial information about the junta and its activities and secret documents were exposed by women, like the AFRC's clandestine arms deal and smuggling of diamonds. The radio station inflamed anti-junta sentiments, keeping civil society united in its protest by blaming the pain and suffering of the people on the AFRC. Women talked about sanctions and the tyranny of the junta. They organized protest demonstrations and sang protest songs. All these concerted efforts of women in exile and those who stayed contributed significantly to sustaining anti-junta civil disobedience.

Protest created mounting pressure on West African states to intervene, and on 10 March 1998 the democratically elected government was reinstated. The struggle, however, continued and women's strength of character and commitment to peace and democracy were again tested by the 6 January 1999 invasion of Freetown by RUF and AFRC rebels. In the wake of the invasion, women participated in the delivery of humanitarian assistance. Freetown as a whole was under siege and it became a fierce battleground between pro-government and RUF/AFRC forces. The imperative for peace became more compelling than ever. Women initiated frequent meetings to strategize on how to get the parties to the negotiating table. They participated in the National Consultative Conference convened by Dr Kadi Sesay, chair of the National Commission for Democracy and Human Rights, which was given the mandate to collate civil society's views on the peace talks to be held in Lomé. Women, as well as other civil society leaders, participated with keen interest in the conference and expressed legitimate concerns on issues of blanket amnesty, which had the potential of perpetuating impunity for grave crimes, and a government of national unity, which could set the precedent that crime pays.[19]

Despite the determinant role they played in ending violence in Sierra Leone, women were under-represented when the time came to discuss peace. Women were outnumbered by men at the Lomé peace talks. They were not even given the opportunity to sign the historic Lomé Peace Agreement. This is unfortunate, given the invaluable effort of women in achieving peace and democracy. While the fundamental causes of the war were of men's making, and the core founding leaders of the rebel movement were men, one can say that the Lomé Accord was to a very large extent the product of women's struggle for peace. It is a "women's peace", signed by men. The only woman's signature was that of the Organization of African Unity representative, Miss Coleman.

THE ROLE OF WOMEN IN PEACE-BUILDING

At this point in Sierra Leone's political history, to which women have made a significant contribution, the Sierra Leone government continues to deny itself the potential benefit of placing women at strategic decision-making levels. There is not one woman commissioner in the Commission for the Consolidation of Peace. There is no woman at a decision-making level in the National Commission for Reconstruction, Resettlement and Rehabilitation (NCRRR). There are only two female cabinet ministers out of twenty two, three deputy ministers out of thirteen and seven women parliamentarians out of eighty in the new political dispensation of national unity. And there is no woman in the Joint Monitoring Commission or ceasefire monitoring committees. There is no woman in the disarmament sensitization committee—women are completely marginalized from disarmament, which is unfortunate given the tremendous opportunities for women to make it successful.

There will be no sustainable peace in Sierra Leone without a lasting solution to the current unchecked proliferation of small arms and light weapons. Disarmament is not limited to the withdrawal of weapons from combatants, it also entails the creation or establishment of conditions that dissuade or prevent combatants from seeking to acquire weapons again. Since women contributed to the militarization of society by smuggling small arms and light weapons, among other things, they can contribute to the demilitarization process by reversing their actions in a variety of ways. They can stop smuggling weapons, thereby curbing the diffusion of weapons, which is now a social menace. Given the influence and the moral authority of African mothers, they can prevail on their sons through persuasion and sensitization to surrender their weapons, demobilize, and come home.

Women can act as neighbourhood watchdogs for weapons that have been smuggled into communities or hidden by combatants. This role is extremely important because, in addition to AFRC and RUF combatants, who may not surrender all of their weapons, there are thousands of men in the civil militias who were heavily armed by the government for counter-insurgency reasons. It is obvious that not all of them will hand in all their weapons. This scenario poses a national security threat, and will compound Sierra Leone's social problems, because these weapons could be used for armed banditry by idle ex-combatants. Or they could be used for the violent settlement of differences of opinion, and they will certainly increase the risk of domestic violence. Being at home and in their communities most of the time, women are aware of the inner workings of their communities: they can act as "watchwomen" for unknown travellers of evil intent, and for illicit arms transfers among community members.

In addition to helping disarm communities, women have a vital role to play in the liberation of the human spirit, by rehabilitating and reconciling people and communities. By using traditional trauma counselling skills and mediation strategies, women can disarm the minds of victims and perpetrators. They have an especially important role to play in the rehabilitation of child soldiers. By mobilizing community support systems, good neighbourliness, fostered by African communal life, extended family support systems, secret initiation societies, and through community elders, religious elders, education at home and in schools, women can liberate the minds of child combatants who, at a very impressionable age, have been exposed to the most outrageous form of violence. Women are best placed to perform this role because they spend more time with children, and above all because of their natural role in binding society and carrying and nurturing life.

Women can serve as therapists for children and other victims because they are good listeners. And they can empathize since they themselves suffer social injustice. Women can listen to children explain the horrors they have experienced; they can give children love and hope, something abused children desperately need. Women can talk with the children, make them feel secure and wanted, give children the love and moral support they need to understand that the world is not full of demons. Women can act as agents of reconciliation and rehabilitation in their communities. They must disarm the minds of victims who, for understandable reasons, may want to take revenge. Women can encourage people to forgive, if not to forget; and persuade others not to avenge the brutal death, senseless killings, maiming and slaughter of their loved ones. And women can disarm the minds of victimizers, who may want to snap again. By so doing, they can transform the culture of violence that has been perpetuated for almost a decade into a culture of peace.

There is also a role for women as peacemakers through West African civil society. Fully aware of the interdependence of countries in the subregion, Sierra Leonean women can contribute to subregional disarmament by offering their experiences to their West African sisters to enable them to identify potential interfaces for collaboration on conflict prevention, management and peace-building in the interest of the region.

WOMEN AGAINST WEAPONS IN WEST AFRICA: AN AGENDA FOR PEACE-BUILDING

It is the abundance of small arms and light weapons that makes war terrible for women and keeps the risk of violence real. These easily acquired and easily used tools of death have inflicted unspeakable pain and suffering on Sierra Leone's population, and women and children in particular. Even where machetes have been used for mutilation, firearms hold the victim in place. Some weapons were taken from the Sierra Leone military arsenal by renegade soldiers who joined forces with the RUF. Most entered the country through neighbouring countries (Liberia and Guinea mainly). Weapons proliferation from Liberia was easy: Liberia was fully involved in the armed conflict, and the RUF had total control of the Liberia–Sierra Leone border since their headquarters were in Kailahun, in the diamond-rich far east of Sierra Leone.

Women in Sierra Leone (and West Africa) have shown that they are overwhelmingly tired of violence and definitely committed to peace. They can play a determinant role in the fight against small arms and light weapons, but they need a clearly defined plan of action. Here are some basic elements.

- Include women as commissioners in the Commission for the Consolidation of Peace, the NCRRR, the disarmament sensitization committee. They should also be included in the Truth and Reconciliation Commission and the National Commission for Democracy and Human Rights.
- Provide more space for women at all decision-making levels. If women are represented in significant numbers, they can bring alternative concepts to defence and security. They could allocate more money to human security: food, health and economic security are the foundation stones of national security. Full enjoyment of human rights will curb the national security threat from within, and contribute to conflict prevention.
- Build on existing women's organizations and strengthen viable grass-roots women's organizations at community and district level to participate in the consolidation of peace, especially in devastated, war-ravaged zones.
- Provide institutional support and capacity-building to women's organizations—violence is less likely to continue in Sierra Leone if there is capacity across the country for non-violent conflict resolution. Establishing this capacity or increasing its effectiveness is important for peace. Good will and good faith are not enough.
- Support and promote networking between national women's organizations, local women's organizations and other agencies, to share experiences and collaborate on peace-building programmes.
- Support and encourage women's organizations to promote dialogue between women from warring factions: this can open up alternative routes to conflict resolution and reconciliation and confidence-building. Informal dialogue will encourage aggressors and victims to understand opposing views, and dispel negative stereotypes.
- Support organizations like the Campaign for Good Governance (CGG) and other women-led organizations working with the grass roots to engage them in the governance of the country. Peace and security depend on viable democratic institutions. CGG's mission

statement is "to encourage and facilitate the full and genuine participation of all Sierra Leoneans in the democratic processes of the country". This gives people a sense of ownership of the process of governance, the lack of which contributed to the destruction of the country. It will also enable the electorate to identify and vote for politicians with a good political agenda and to kick out the corrupt ones. It is significant to note that women have a democratic advantage in reshaping the political landscape of Sierra Leone: they outnumber men, many of whom died in the war.

- Build women's capacity to identify early warning signs for conflict, which may have the potential of escalating, destabilizing communities.

- Strengthen the grass roots, where participation in the democratic process is at an all-time high. Women's organizations need resources and logistics to sustain this momentum by continuously engaging the grass roots in participatory democratic governance.

- Rehabilitate traditional mediation skills. In the aftermath of the brutal war, which destroyed many communities, support should be given to women for settling disputes under the *palava* tree. We need to mobilize community meetings, secret initiation societies, community elders, and the moral authority and influence of mothers and aunts.

- Enhance the role of women leaders in national and international peace-building. This can be done by giving women access to important decision-making institutions and mechanisms to develop their knowledge of conflict resolution and to establish mechanisms that provide decision makers with inputs from the grass roots.

- Organize workshops, seminars or meetings for women's organizations and women pioneers to enhance their understanding of the moratorium on small arms and light weapons signed by ECOWAS heads of state on 31 October 1998. They in turn can then develop and implement sensitization and persuasion programmes in the local media (radio, TV, press) as well as conduct field missions to communities to disseminate the rationale of the moratorium. This should highlight the link between the proliferation and diffusion of small arms and light weapons and the experiences of child combatants. Women pioneers might start campaigning for a moratorium on toy weapons, which have the potential of exposing children (who have already been exposed to an appalling scale of violence) to more violence.

- Organize workshops, seminars or meetings for women's organizations, wives of ex-combatants to be included, on the role they can play in disarmament. The indiscriminate availability of small arms and light weapons should be related to the gender-specific experiences these women have gone through. The workshops should address the psychotherapeutic role women can play in peace-building by using their rich traditional mediation skills—as was done in Mali—instead of relying on Western psychotherapy skills: these may not be appropriate to their needs, and in any case require resources that are not easily forthcoming. As seen earlier, women are crucial to enhance the reconciliation process both for individuals and communities.

- Support and encourage subregional and regional solidarity and networking between women's organizations in Sierra Leone and neighbouring countries. Some have gone through similar experiences: Sierra Leone can learn from the reconciliation processes of northern Mali and northern Ghana. And Sierra Leone's women may have experiences they can share in countries where there is a risk of armed conflict.

How can we organize collectively, in order to survive? How can we curb internal and cross-border proliferation of small arms and light weapons through our porous borders?

A significant number of countries in the region are experiencing instability of one kind or the other. Sierra Leone and Liberia have experienced brutal war. Guinea and Côte d'Ivoire have shown signs of political instability. Togo and Benin have experienced serious social and political problems. Nigeria harbours ethnic and religious conflicts that are threatening national and regional security. An explosion in one of these countries could have spillover effects similar to those of the Liberian conflict in Sierra Leone. West African women should come together and join forces to fight the scourges of armed conflict, small arms and light weapons at a subregional level.

The framework presented above comes from deep reflection on the Sierra Leonean experience. It is not a pretentious attempt to show that what works for Sierra Leone can work for all West African states. Let it serve rather as a mirror for our sisters to look at and identify areas of commonality. Let a reflection emanating from our sufferings and successes instruct and inspire others in their aspirations for peace, security and democracy.

The framework could stimulate our West African sisters to create a "Network of Women Against Weapons in West Africa", with a vision of ensuring our survival as a group by achieving peace and stability, but also—and most importantly for everyone living in the region—with a vision of a life free from that violence that strips men and women of their human dignity.

Notes

1   *The Washington Post*, 11 April 2000.
2   Women who have gone on pilgrimage to Mecca are revered by the less fortunate. Many underprivileged women are not lucky enough to have their lifetime dream of going to Mecca come true.
3   The PL480 (Public Law 480) is American rice aid given to Sierra Leone in order for the government to sell it at a very low price for the benefit of the people. The proceeds were to be used as soft loans for funding domestic development programmes.
4   Another face of the fate of women in pre-war Sierra Leone is what came to be known as the "Sugar Daddy" culture. This was a way of life for politicians who would lure young girls—especially schoolgirls and young women, offering money and their political status in exchange for sexual favours. Some of these schoolgirls, who could not afford to further their education due to poverty generated by corruption, yielded to the temptation of the politicians and other rich businessmen they called "Sugar Daddies" in order to get money to pay fees, feed their families and clothe themselves.
5   Interview.
6   Testimony of Sia Lebbie of Jaiama Sewafe on 20 February 2000.
7   Sulaiman Momodu and Chris Samai in *Concord Times*, 27 September 1995.
8   Data of sexual abuse collected between the period of March 1999–January 2000 by the Forum for African Women Educationalists in collaboration with Médecins Sans Frontières Holland, the Ministry of

Social Welfare, Gender and Children Affairs, UNICEF and the Sierra Leone Association of University Women.

9   *Sierra Leone Newsletter*, Vol. 3, No. 3, 1998, p. 6.

10   Sulaiman Momodu in *Concord Times*, 1 June 1998.

11   Testimony of Saladeen Fuad, a Civil Defence Unit member, on 18 February 2000.

12   *Concord Times*, 23 June 1998, p. 1.

13   "Structural violence" has been defined by Johan Galtung "as social and personal violence arising from unjust, repressive and oppressive, national or international, political and social structures. According to this view, a system that generates repression, abject poverty, malnutrition, and starvation for some members of a society while other members enjoy opulence and unbridled power inflicts covert violence, except that it does it in more subtle ways. In other words, it is not only the gun that kills. Lack of access to basic means of life and dignity does the same thing". See Hizkias Assefa, *Peace and Reconciliation as a Paradigm—A Philosophy of Peace and its Implications on Conflict, Governance, and Economic Growth in Africa*, Nairobi, 1993.

14   Quoted in Isatou Gibrill, *Gender Politics and Democratization 1992– 1997*, Freetown, 1998, p. 26.

15   Ibid.

16   Ibid.

17   "Women's position paper on the forthcoming General Election dated 6 February 1996", Freetown, 1996.

18   Press release for the Sierra Leone Women's Forum. Not dated. Another press release from Bintumani 2 advising women: "Remember, you must be registered to vote … make sure you, your family and your friends are registered". The same press release goes on: "We the women renew our plea to Foday Sankoh and the RUF to work with us in rebuilding a peaceful and democratic Sierra Leone. We call for a ceasefire on Election Day and thereafter. Let peace reign".

19   However, these views were compromised in Lomé, because of the exigencies of the negotiations. It was a painful moment for all civil society participants in the peace negotiations. Eventually, all combatants were granted amnesty, and a government of national unity was formed, including the rebels.

CHAPTER 11

A PRICE FOR PEACE? JUSTICE AND RECONCILIATION IN POST-WAR SIERRA LEONE

Joe A. D. Alie

CRIME AND WAR

Sierra Leone is emerging from a decade of civil conflict characterized by horrendous human rights violations. Thousands of defenceless civilians have been killed, tortured or maimed and hundreds of thousands more displaced. Women and girls have been subjected to the most gruesome sexual and other abuse. Young children have been forcibly recruited to perform combatant roles. There has been massive infrastructure destruction, especially in the provincial areas, where towns and villages have been completely destroyed. The economy is in ruins. Human Rights Watch summed up the situation thus: "Sierra Leone's nine-year conflict was characterized by unspeakable brutality. International war crimes of the worst type were routinely and systematically committed against Sierra Leoneans of all ages. The suffering inflicted upon the civilian population has been profound. While all sides committed human rights violations, rebel forces were responsible for the overwhelming majority."[1]

The rebels used terror tactics to abduct men, women and children into their ranks and to devastate the countryside. One may ask why the Revolutionary United Front (RUF) rebels unleashed an avalanche of terror on the very people they said they had set out to liberate? It would appear that, despite their revolutionary rhetoric, the RUF fighters were more interested in looting and carnage than in creating a utopia in Sierra Leone where exploitation of "man by man" would be a thing of the past.

It has been suggested that the mercenaries recruited by the RUF were largely responsible for the atrocities committed. Those from Liberia, in particular, shared very little of the ideology of the RUF. Richards put it this way: "… Liberian mercenaries, preoccupied with the logistics of looting, and carrying out atrocities against undefended villagers, frittered away any initial strategic advantage, and lost the movement (RUF) any local sympathy it might otherwise have gathered."[2] Be that as it may, the RUF atrocities continued and escalated even after the Liberian and other mercenaries had left the movement. Interviews with former rebel fighters and accounts by former hostages (abductees) reveal a startling characteristic of the RUF rebels—killing and maiming without any remorse.

The RUF campaign took a new turn on 25 May 1997, when segments of the Sierra Leone Army (SLA) staged a *coup d'état* and overthrew the democratically elected government of President Ahmad Tejan Kabbah. The junta called on the RUF leadership to join ranks with them in forming a new administration—the Armed Forces Revolutionary Council (AFRC). The rebel leadership not only accepted the invitation but went ahead and merged its fighters with the rebellious soldiers to create what they termed the "People's Army". One of the first major pronouncements of the AFRC was that peace had finally come to Sierra Leone. According to them, the merger of the SLA and the RUF meant, among other things, that the former enemies (i.e. the government soldiers and the RUF rebels) no longer saw themselves as antagonists. As such the war in Sierra Leone had effectively ended.

In reality, the peace promised by the AFRC and its rebel allies turned out to be an illusion. The nine months of AFRC rule (May 1997–February 1998) was one of the most trying periods in the country's post-independence history. The coup was universally condemned in Sierra Leone and abroad. Most Sierra Leoneans and the international community refused to recognize the regime or to do business with it. Patriotic Sierra Leoneans mounted a very effective civil disobedience campaign against the AFRC, which virtually paralysed the junta's activities.

Realizing that it did not have the support of the people, the junta resorted to terror tactics in order to cow Sierra Leoneans into submission. Violence and insecurity followed the military coup and many people lost their lives. Amnesty International said:

> Since a military coup on 25 May 1997, in which the Government of
> President Ahmad Tejan Kabbah was overthrown, the rule of law in Sierra
> Leone has completely collapsed … Since the military coup soldiers,

together with members of the RUF who have joined forces with them, have committed serious human rights violations ... Lack of effective control over both soldiers and members of the RUF has resulted in human rights violations being committed with impunity. Hundreds of people have been arbitrarily arrested and detained; many have been tortured and ill-treated. Physical assault, amounting to ill-treatment, of civilians by soldiers and members of the RUF is routine. There have also been reports of extra-judicial executions of some of those suspected of opposing the AFRC.[3]

Ill-treatment of opponents and suspected opponents of the military led to the flight from the country of many intellectuals and professionals—judges, lawyers, lecturers, some senior military and police officers, civil servants and other public sector workers. Junta soldiers did not hesitate to kill. They even assassinated a 90-year-old paramount chief, Albert Sandy Demby, father of the ousted vice-president, Dr Albert Joe Demby. Chief Demby was killed in his home town, Baoma, on 26 June 1997.

Women and young girls particularly suffered at the hands of the AFRC. A woman from the southern provincial town of Bo commented thus:

We tried to make peace with them [AFRC] to save lives and further destruction. Each day we fed them rice from our own pots, we prayed with them; Christian with Christian, Muslim with Muslim, and what did they do—they turned on us again. They raped, they robbed, they burnt, they killed. They are not sorry, they would do it again. How can we forgive that?

In February 1998 the Economic Community of West African States' Monitoring Group (ECOMOG), together with civil militia groups, succeeded in terminating the rule of the AFRC, and constitutional order was again restored. But the crisis was not over. While ECOMOG secured most of the major towns including Freetown, the AFRC/RUF fighters entrenched themselves in many parts of the Eastern and Northern Provinces, where they unleashed a new wave of terror under code names such as "operation no living thing" and "operation pay yourself". They embarked on a large-scale policy of human mutilation. On the other side, between February and April 1998, civilians claiming to be in opposition to the AFRC acted as vigilantes, often killing persons alleged to be junta or junta collaborators, and destroying their property.

On 6 January 1999 the AFRC and their RUF allies made another desperate attempt to capture the capital city, Freetown, and overthrow the government. The rebels came within a whisker of taking over the city, but were repelled by ECOMOG, at considerable cost. This latest rebel onslaught underlined how difficult it is to defeat this kind of rebellion militarily, particularly as it became clear that the rebels were being heavily supported by Liberia and one or two other West African countries.[4] It became imperative for the two sides (government and AFRC) to get together in dialogue and negotiation before the entire country was laid waste.[5]

Many local organizations and individual Sierra Leoneans now began openly to support the government's call for dialogue with the rebels. For instance, the National Commission for Democracy and Human Rights (NCDHR), while condemning the "terrible carnage, widespread arson, wanton abduction and rape of women, girls and even pregnant women; the indiscriminate maiming, torture and abduction of children, youths and the aged ... calls unequivocally on all the people of Sierra Leone to renew their commitment to peace and democracy by actively supporting the peace process already initiated by the Government ... and to which the AFRC/RUF have given cautious welcome". In a similar vein, the Sierra Leone Human Rights Community (an umbrella organization of various local human rights groups in Sierra Leone) expressed "its support for the recent policy of the Sierra Leone Government to actively pursue dialogue in its search for a lasting solution of the crisis".

The chairman of the National Consultative Conference on the Peace Process, Professor Victor Strasser-King, put it this way: "The invasion of Freetown by the SLA/RUF/AFRC alliance has intensified the call for peace almost to the point of near hysteria. Every sector of Sierra Leone society is now part of the peace movement. Today almost all Sierra Leoneans have a common objective: peace to our country. What however is still contentious, is the mode of achieving this common objective."

One Sierra Leonean, who was very sceptical about these calls for peace with the rebels, sounded a cautionary note: "The opportunity for peace in Sierra Leone is already mirage; we Sierra Leoneans are not yet ready for peace; we are not honest and sincere about peace; the country is regrettably divided on the peace process; there is no love to hold us together; we are not a nation state; we have selfishly failed to constitute a common front to this crisis that has continued to ruin the social fabric of our society, rather, we are individuals, we are tribes, we are regions and we are politicians."[6]

CRIME AND PUNISHMENT

One of the most controversial issues Sierra Leone will have to face on the long road to peace is what to do with war crimes and war criminals in the post-conflict era. This issue is essentially about the question of *amnesty*, which is central to the peace process. The issue of amnesty, like the disarmament, demobilization and reintegration (DDR) programme, is central to the peace process in Sierra Leone.

Bu-Buakei Jabbi[7] postulates that in resolving large-scale conflicts involving gross atrocities, the reconciliatory force of amnesty may commend itself as a plausible political option. He suggests two kinds of amnesty: retrospective amnesty and prospective amnesty. Retrospective amnesty is the prerogative of mercy provided for in certain constitutions. It gives the head of state the power to pardon a person *after* having been judged guilty of a specified offence by judicial due process of law. Retrospective amnesty does not, however, apply to civil wrongs.

Such a prerogative is provided for in Section 63 (1) of the Sierra Leone Constitution (1991). The relevant section, entitled "Prerogative of Mercy", reads as follows:

(1) The President may, acting in accordance with the advice of a Committee appointed by the Cabinet over which the Vice President shall preside:
    (a) Grant any person convicted of any offence against the laws of Sierra Leone a pardon, either free or subject to lawful conditions;
    (b) Grant to any person a respite, either indefinite or for a specified period of the execution of any punishment imposed on that person for such an offence;
    (c) Substitute a less severe form of punishment for any punishment imposed on any person for such an offence;
    (d) Remit the whole or any part of any punishment imposed upon any person for such an offence or any penalty or forfeiture otherwise due to the Government on account of such an offence.

Prospective amnesty is quite different: it is essentially waiving, *before* the event, any future prosecution of persons presumed to have committed criminal offences or civil wrongs, thereby pre-empting or short-circuiting the usual due process of law for determining guilt or liability. This form of amnesty has serious legal, moral and political implications. For instance, legally, it may run counter to certain international conventions on humanitarian law, war crimes or genocide, that Sierra Leone may have signed.

It is prospective amnesty that we are concerned with in this paper. The granting of retrospective amnesty by the head of state is not questionable in law. It is the right of the head of the state, granted by the country's constitution. We may note that President Tejan Kabbah, shortly after the signing of the Lomé Peace Agreement on 7 July 1999, granted amnesty to all AFRC/RUF men and women, together with their sympathizers, who had been found guilty of various offences against the state.

As far as the issue of peace and justice are concerned, Sierra Leoneans are placed between a rock and hard place. One school is of the view that if we want to achieve sustainable peace in Sierra Leone, a blanket amnesty must be granted to the AFRC/RUF and their allies. Others disagree. We shall consider each in turn.

IN FAVOUR OF AMNESTY: REASONS AND ARGUMENTS

- A blanket amnesty will facilitate the process of reconciliation and healing. Put differently, it is important to look to the future during this critical peace process. Let bygones be bygones. It is argued that in Mozambique, reconciliation was achieved without digging up the horrors of the past.
- The rebels will not feel ostracized by society. They will be encouraged to come out of the bush without fear of reprisals.
- Article 14 of the Abidjan Peace Accord of 30 November 1996 conferred amnesty on all perpetrators of human rights violations during the rebel war. It stated: "To consolidate the peace and promote the cause of national reconciliation, the Government of Sierra Leone shall ensure that no official or judicial action is taken against any member of the RUF/SL in respect of anything done by them in pursuit of their objectives as members of that organization up to the time of the signing of this Agreement. In addition, legislative and other measures necessary to guarantee former RUF/SL combatants, exiles and other persons currently outside the

country for reasons related to the armed conflict shall be adopted ensuring the full exercise of their civil and political rights, with a view to their reintegration within a framework of full legality." Since the Government of Sierra Leone and civil society groups had agreed to use the Abidjan Peace Accord as the basis for future dialogue with the rebels, it was only rational that the amnesty granted to the rebels in Abidjan should be maintained.

- During the negotiations leading to the signing of the Abidjan Peace Accord, the government was bargaining from a position of strength. But since then the situation had changed dramatically in favour of the rebels, and therefore any insistence on the part of the government to institute legal proceedings against the RUF would result in the collapse of the peace talks. Civilians would continue to suffer abduction, abuse and death at the hands of the RUF. The number of internally displaced persons and refugees would continue to swell. A collapse of the peace agreement would be in the interest of the RUF, as they would continue to control large portions of the most economically viable areas of the country, including the diamond mining areas.

- Finally, a blanket amnesty for the rebels is justified on the grounds that it is extremely difficult to ascertain the level of atrocities committed by each member of the RUF and their allies. There would be the added problem of getting witnesses willing to testify against the rebels: during the 6 January 1999 invasion of Freetown, some of the AFRC members directed their anger at those who had previously testified against their colleagues, and they moved particularly against the police.

Article IX of the Lomé Peace Agreement accordingly offers blanket amnesty to the RUF, AFRC and others. It states:

- In order to bring lasting peace to Sierra Leone, the Government of Sierra Leone shall take appropriate legal steps to grant Corporal Foday Sankoh absolute and free pardon.

- After the signing of the present Agreement, the Government of Sierra Leone shall also grant absolute and free pardon and reprieve to all combatants and collaborators in respect of anything done by them in pursuit of their objectives, up to the time of the signing of the present Agreement.

– To consolidate the peace and promote the cause of national reconciliation, the Government of Sierra Leone shall ensure that no official or judicial action is taken against any member of the RUF/SL, ex-AFRC (Armed Forces Revolutionary Council), ex-SLA (Sierra Leone Army) or CDF (Civil Defence Forces) in respect of anything done by them in pursuit of their objectives, as members of those organizations, since March 1991, up to the time of the signing of the present Agreement. In addition, legislative and other measures necessary to guarantee immunity to former combatants, exiles and other persons, currently outside the country for reasons related to the armed conflict, shall be adopted ensuring the full exercise of their civil and political rights, with a view to their reintegration within a framework of full legality.

One important thing to note is that those who advocate a blanket amnesty for the rebels and advance the above arguments do not necessarily want peace *at any cost*.

AGAINST AMNESTY: REASONS AND ARGUMENTS

- Conflict cannot be resolved, and peace cannot be attained, unless we pay attention to fairness and justice of the process as well as to the outcome. In other words, peace without justice is meaningless. Justice is a precondition for reconciliation. If the victims of human rights abuses are denied justice, they may take the law into their own hands and seek retribution. A blanket amnesty, the argument goes, does not therefore augur well for national unity and reconciliation.
- A blanket amnesty will allow the perpetrators of some of the most heinous crimes to go unpunished and will not deter future human rights violations. Allowing the violators of human rights to walk free merely encourages others to commit similar or worse crimes in the future. The impunity of political leaders has troubled Sierra Leoneans for three decades. How will the cycle of impunity be broken without some form of censure or punishment for the worst offenders?
- Rwanda is a case of failed of amnesty: in 1959 certain Rwandans are believed to have committed gross human rights violations in their country. They went unpunished partly because the people desired peace and did not wish to open up old wounds. The result was that the cycle of violence was repeated in 1994: within the space of three months, nearly one million Rwandans were

massacred. It is argued that if the 1959 culprits had been punished, the genocide of 1994 might not have taken place.

- A blanket amnesty violates certain provisions of the Sierra Leone Constitution. Consequently, such an amnesty would not contribute to the preservation of our fledgling democracy. The former chair of the National Commission for Democracy and Human Rights, Dr Kadi Sesay, summed it up in the following words: "In our present predicament our national integrity may indeed require us to make sacrifices, concessions and adjustments in the cause of peace ... However, it is our duty to point out that a new democratic nation can only be rebuilt on a firm constitutional foundation ... There is no sustainable peace without justice."

- It is doubtful whether any amnesty granted by the president or Parliament will be valid under international law. The International Covenant on Civil and Political Rights, which Sierra Leone ratified in 1996, prohibits the enactment of blanket amnesty laws, and so do the Geneva Conventions. Any blanket amnesty, it is argued, will violate Sierra Leone's obligations under these and other international laws. The legality of a blanket amnesty could be challenged in a Sierra Leone court of law and such litigation might polarize society further.

- The violation of human rights is of grave concern to the international community as well as to Sierra Leoneans. For instance, United Nations High Commissioner for Human Rights Mary Robinson, Amnesty International, Human Rights Watch and other bodies have vehemently condemned the atrocities committed by the rebels and their allies. During Mary Robinson's visit to Sierra Leone in June 1999 a Human Rights Manifesto for Sierra Leone was published. Signatories of the manifesto declared and reaffirmed their commitment to the unwavering and non-discriminatory promotion of all human rights for present and future generations in Sierra Leone. Paragraph four of the document reiterated that "the people of Sierra Leone seek peace with justice and respect for human rights".

- War crimes trials, the trials of persons charged with criminal violation of the laws and customs of war and related principles of international law, are becoming established legal practice. After the Second World War a series of trials were held in Europe. The Nuremberg Trials in Germany had the authority of two legal instruments. One, the London Agreement, was signed by representatives of the United States, the United Kingdom, France and the Soviet Union in London on 8 August 1945; the other, Law No. 10, was promulgated by the Allied Control Council in Berlin on 20 December 1945. The London Agreement provided for the establishment of an International Military Tribunal to try war criminals. Under the London Agreement, defendants were charged under three broad categories:

– Crimes against peace, that is, crimes involving the planning, initiating, and waging of aggressive war;
– War crimes, that is, violations of the laws and customs of war as embodied in the Hague Conventions; and
– Crimes against humanity, such as the extermination of racial, ethnic and religious groups and other large-scale atrocities against civilians.

It may be recalled that in 1993 and 1994 the United Nations established war crimes tribunals to prosecute those who committed crimes during the civil wars in the former Yugoslavia and in Rwanda. More recently, efforts have been made to try the former military dictator of Chile, Augusto Pinochet, in Spain even though the Chilean constitution, which was written by Pinochet's government, protects him from being prosecuted for crimes carried out during his dictatorship. Discussions are presently under way at the United Nations concerning the proposed trial of leaders of the former Khmer Rouge regime in Cambodia. Another recent example relates to the ex-president of Chad, Hissein Habre, who had taken refuge in Senegal. Chadians are in the process of filing suits against Habre for gross human rights abuses during his rule. There is no reason for Sierra Leone to be an exception.

THE COMPROMISE:
A TRUTH AND RECONCILIATION COMMISSION

The significance of granting a blanket amnesty to the RUF/AFRC as part of the price Sierra Leone would have to pay for peace was not lost on the rebel leadership. One of the key issues in the RUF's proposals to the government for discussion at the Lomé peace talks related to amnesty for the rebels. Recall that Foday Sankoh had been accused of treason and sentenced to death in 1998. He had appealed against his sentence and judgement on the appeal was pending when the AFRC/RUF hit Freetown in January 1999. In their proposals, the rebels called for the unconditional release of their leader, Corporal Foday Sankoh, as well as the granting of an amnesty to the AFRC and their collaborators.

The government's position on these two interrelated issues was unequivocal. On the issue of the unconditional release of Foday Sankoh, the government stated that "President Kabbah has always said that he would not hesitate to grant Corporal Foday Sankoh his freedom within the judicial and constitutional process, if this is the price to be paid for lasting peace in Sierra Leone". Regarding amnesty to the AFRC and their collaborators, the government response was that "as in the case of Corporal Foday Sankoh, amnesty for this category of persons will be examined with a view to achieving permanent peace in Sierra Leone. The government will however take into consideration gross human rights violations committed against the citizens of this country, and the attitude of Sierra Leoneans and the international community to the perpetrators of such violence".

The Lomé Peace Agreement granted absolute and free pardon and reprieve to all combatants and their collaborators in respect of anything done by them in pursuit of their objectives from March 1991 to 7 July 1999 (Article IX of the Lomé Peace Agreement). But the issue of impunity, justice and reconciliation was not ignored. It was proposed that a Truth and Reconciliation Commission (TRC) be established within ninety days of signing the agreement.

Article XXVI of the Lomé Peace Agreement says in part that:

A Truth and Reconciliation Commission shall be established to address impunity, break the cycle of violence, provide a forum for both the victims and perpetrators of human rights violations to tell their story, get a clear picture of the past in order to facilitate genuine healing and reconciliation. In the spirit of national reconciliation, the Commission shall deal with the question of human rights violations since the beginning of the Sierra Leone conflict in 1991. The Commission shall, among other things, recommend measures to be taken for the rehabilitation of victims of human rights violations.

Truth commissions have been increasing in number in recent years. These commissions grow out of transitional dynamics "to confront, record, and acknowledge the truth about a past period of widespread rights abuses, with the hope of contributing to reconciliation, healing and reform".[8] These commissions are created on the premise that "every society has the inalienable right to know the truth about past events and about the circumstances and reasons which led, through the consistent pattern of gross violations of human rights, to the perpetration of aberrant crimes. Full and effective exercise of the right to the truth is essential to avoid any recurrence of such acts in the future".

Soon after the signing of the Lomé Accord, various international human rights organizations, including Human Rights Watch, began to put pressure on the government to set up the Truth and Reconciliation Commission. It would appear that while the international community generally was anxious to have the commission established, the Government of Sierra Leone and a large section of the Sierra Leone populace were not too keen on its immediate establishment.[9]

In the first place, the disarmament process has been moving at a very slow pace. Combatants have been very reluctant to disarm, partly because the structures necessary to facilitate their disarmament have not been put in place. More importantly, there is still considerable mistrust of the government by the RUF/AFRC leadership. It is also feared that the TRC might adversely affect disarmament, if it were set up at the beginning of the disarmament process. Rebel groups might hesitate to emerge from the bush for fear of being arraigned before what they would perceive as a court of law. The government position, supported by most people, is "to make haste slowly".

THE APPLICATION OF JUSTICE

There appears to be some problem in the application of justice following the signing of the Lomé Peace Agreement. Human rights organizations, particularly Human Rights Watch, are anxious that the Truth and Reconciliation Commission (TRC) and its complementary, quasi-judicial body, the Human Rights Commission, be set up without further delay as provided for in the peace agreement. These two bodies were supposed to be set up within ninety days of the signing of the agreement: this means that by October 1999 both bodies should have been in operation.

In its letter of 23 January 2000 to Modibo Sidibe, Minister of Foreign Affairs of the Republic of Mali and Chairperson of the Joint Implementation Committee of the agreement (Article XXXII of the Lomé Peace Agreement), Human Rights Watch (which had meticulously documented human rights abuses by the RUF, AFRC and ECOMOG since the signing of the agreement) pointed out that "these violations are no longer covered under the general amnesty and must be treated as criminal offences punishable under Sierra Leonean law". Consequently, the organization called on the RUF and AFRC leadership to initiate criminal investigations into followers who had perpetrated crimes against the civilian population. The letter goes on to state that there appears "to be a general reluctance on the part of the authorities to establish the rule of law, or investigate and arrest individual rebels responsible for these crimes. We have learned that on several occasions authorities have decided not to make such arrests 'in the name of reconciliation'. We believe such a reaction only serves to undermine the rule of law and sabotage any future peace for Sierra Leone".

This letter poses a real dilemma for the government and ordinary citizens. The government and certain sections of the civilian population would like to institute criminal proceedings against the human rights violators, but there are genuine fears that such action, though understandable, might jeopardize the fragile peace process. Government and law enforcement agencies privately admit that it would have been much easier to prosecute these offenders if the DDR programme had been almost completed. But, by the time of writing, only about twenty per cent of combatants (out of an estimated 45,000) had been disarmed. How can the perpetrators of crimes be brought to book when they are still at large and are heavily armed? Any attempt to use force to bring them into line could backfire, and might lead to a resumption of hostilities. And nobody wants that.

The situation has not been helped by RUF leader Foday Sankoh's declarations to the international press that he sees no need for, and will instruct his troops not to participate in, the Truth and Reconciliation Commission. If Sankoh is not inclined to cooperate with the TRC (which is not going to be a tribunal), one cannot see how the RUF will accept the jurisdiction of a court that has powers to punish law-breakers. Sankoh's uncompromising stance would seem to indicate that despite his verbal pronouncements that he and his men are sorry for their actions over the past decade, he feels no genuine remorse.

Finally, on 22 February 2000 the Sierra Leone Parliament enacted The Truth and Reconciliation Commission Act. The commission shall consist of seven members: four shall be citizens of Sierra Leone and the rest shall be non-citizens; all shall be appointed by the president from among persons recommended by the UN Special Representative of the Secretary-General in Sierra Leone and the UN High Commissioner for Human Rights.

OBJECTIVE AND FUNCTIONS OF THE COMMISSION

The objective of the TRC is:

- to create an impartial historical record of violations and abuses of human rights and international humanitarian law related to the armed conflict in Sierra Leone, from the beginning of the conflict in 1991 to the signing of the Lomé Peace Agreement;
- to address impunity, to respond to the needs of victims;
- to promote healing and reconciliation; and
- to prevent a repetition of the violations and abuses suffered.

The commission's functions are as follows:

- to investigate and report on the causes, nature, and extent of the violations and abuses referred to above to the fullest degree possible, including their antecedents, the context in which violations and abuses occurred, the question of whether those violations and abuses were the result of deliberate planning, policy or authorization by any government, group or individual, and the role of both internal and external factors in the conflict;
- to work to help restore the human dignity of victims and promote reconciliation by providing an opportunity for victims to give an account of the violations and abuses suffered and for perpetrators to relate their experiences, and by creating a climate that fosters constructive interchange between victims and perpetrators, giving special attention to the subject of sexual abuse and to the experiences of children within the armed conflict; and
- to do all such things as may contribute to the fulfilment of the object of the commission.

WHAT TYPE OF JUSTICE DO SIERRA LEONEANS WANT TODAY?

In this highly sensitive period of transition from war to peace, Sierra Leoneans are painfully aware of certain realities.

- Dead relatives and loved ones will never be brought back to life.
- Those women and girls who have been raped and abused in other ways will forever live with the physical pain and emotional trauma associated with such acts.
- People whose limbs have been cut off will forever remain deformed.
- Most people will never be able to regain their lost or damaged possessions.
- Continued violence and instability do not lead to progress.
- What has been done cannot be undone; people must look forward, toward the reconstruction of Sierra Leone society, which is the only reasonable route to follow.

Knowing that they cannot turn the clock back, Sierra Leoneans are faced with a difficult choice in planning the future: they can opt for retributive justice, or they can choose restitutive justice. What most Sierra Leoneans desire most is restitutive justice, which promotes peace and reconciliation, not retributive justice, which seeks to punish offenders.

If we wanted to apply retributive justice, we would have to try all those accused of gross human rights violations since the beginning of the conflict and punish those found guilty. Few people desire this. As one old man, who had come to Freetown as a refugee from Kono, in the east, put it: "Of what use will it be to me if those who burnt my only house are put in jail? They will not be working for me but for the Government. Putting them in jail will not build a new house for me. No, that kind of punishment will not help." Retributive justice would also create a barrier to reconciliation.

Restitutive justice, on the other hand, aims to repair and restore, not to punish. It involves, among other things, an acknowledgement by the wrongdoers of their crimes or actions, an apology to those who have been wronged and a genuine expression of remorse. It also means assisting the victims to cope with their plight through properly planned and well-executed reconstruction and rehabilitation programmes. Articles XXVIII–XXX in the Lomé Peace Agreement provide for such assistance:

Article XXVIII

Post-War Rehabilitation and Reconstruction

(1) The Government, through the National Commission for Resettlement, Rehabilitation and Reconstruction and with the support of the international community, shall provide appropriate financial and technical resources for post-war rehabilitation, reconstruction and development;

(2) Given that women have been particularly victimized during the war, special attention shall be accorded to their needs and potentials in formulating and implementing national rehabilitation, reconstruction and development programmes, to enable them to play a central role in the moral, social and physical reconstruction of Sierra Leone.

Article XXIX

Special Fund for War Victims

The Government, with the support of the international community, shall design and implement a programme for the rehabilitation of war victims. For this purpose, a special fund shall be set up.

Article XXX

Child Combatants

The Government shall accord particular attention to the issue of child soldiers. It shall, accordingly, mobilize resources, both within the country and from the international community, and especially though the Office of the UN Special Representative for Children in Armed Conflict, UNICEF and other agencies, to address the special needs of these children in the existing disarmament, demobilization and reintegration process.

If restitutive justice is properly pursued, everyone stands to benefit, including the state. Durable peace in the country will enable ordinary citizens to go about their daily lives without fear; they will be able to plan their lives as well as those of their children. Government and citizens will be able to make a fresh start rebuilding the economy and society. Resources hitherto spent on the war effort will be available for more productive purposes, such as providing much-needed social services. The country will be able to strengthen its public institutions, both at the central and local levels, thereby making them more responsive to the needs of the people. This task requires strong national leadership and a clear sense of direction, as well as the commitment and total support of the citizens.

The ex-combatants have a big role to play too. They must be persuaded to accept a share of the responsibility to reconstruct the state. At the community level, they could be engaged in projects focused on the construction of roads, bridges and public buildings (e.g. markets, court *barris*, clinics). This active commitment to reconstructing their own lives, and that of the villages, could make their reintegration into communities much easier. Given the resilience of Sierra Leoneans, and their determination to consolidate the peace and move ahead, the prospects for economic and social revival are good.

CONCLUSION

After a decade of carnage and wanton destruction of our human and material resources, we Sierra Leoneans desire peace more than anything else. We are tired of war and want to rebuild our society. But the peace we desire and cherish will be attained at a high price. We will have to make enormous sacrifices. We will have to come to terms with the reality that vengeance cannot lead to sustainable peace. The desire for retributive justice must give way to the greater desire to achieve restitutive justice. We will have to live and interact with the very people who have brought so much suffering on us.

What kind of peace do we want?

Peace is much more than the silencing of guns, the absence of war or violence. It is much more than a condition of tranquillity or a state of calm and serenity. Peace exists "when we feel good with ourselves and with life, even if life or someone has hurt us". Justice is an integral part of peace for, as Hizkias Assefa puts it: "It is not possible to resolve conflicts and attain peace unless attention is given to the justice and fairness of the process as well as the outcome of the settlement." Peace and justice are therefore two sides of the same coin. The real test of peace in Sierra Leone will come when the "chickens come home to roost"[10]: that is, when the former RUF and SLA fighters return to their communities after demobilization. The sufferings of the victims of gross human rights abuses during the war will be greatly reduced if serious attention is paid to their general welfare, not just to the welfare of the ex-combatants.

I would like to conclude with a peace poem written by Amanda Bradley, a Sierra Leonean high-school student:

Peace will come when people live
In friendship, side by side,
And cherish understanding
More than hatred, greed, and pride.

Peace will come when people see
All people as the same,
And no one has to live in fear,
In ignorance or shame.

Peace will come when people
Who are needy can reach out
For shelter, food, or love
And no one has to do without.

Peace will come when people
Learn to listen and to care
About the rights and dignity
Of people everywhere.

Peace will come
When love and trust
And kindness know rebirth,
And on that day all people
Will rejoice in peace on Earth.

Notes

1   Human Rights Watch, "Letter to Mr. Modibo Sidibe, Minister of Foreign Affairs of the Republic of Mali and Chairperson of the Joint Implementation Committee (of the Abidjan Peace Agreement)", Africa Division, 23 January 2000.

2   Paul Richards et al, "Reintegration of War-Affected Youth and Ex-Combatants—A study of the social and economic opportunity structure in Sierra Leone. Report to the Ministry of National

Reconstruction, Resettlement and Rehabilitation", Freetown, November 1996.

3 Amnesty International, "Sierra Leone—A disastrous set-back for human rights", Report, 20 October 1997.

4 A 1999 UN report by Canada's Ambassador Robert Fowler named Burkina Faso and Côte d'Ivoire, as well as diamond dealers including de Beers and the Central Buying Organization in London.

5 See J. B. Laggah, J. A. D. Alie and R. S. V. Wright, "Countries in Conflict: Sierra Leone", in Adebayo Adedeji (ed.), *Comprehending and Mastering African Conflicts—The Search for Sustainable Peace and Good Governance*, London: Zed Books, 1999.

6 See Emmanuel Tom-Rad Kailie, "Sierra Leone: At the Brink of Complete National Disintegration", typescript, June 1999; Kailie analyses why he thinks we are not yet ready for peace in Sierra Leone.

7 Bu-Buakei Jabbi, "Appointive and Political Options in the Peace Process", typescript, Freetown, May 1999.

8 Priscilla B. Hayner, "International Guidelines for the Creation of Truth Commissions: A Preliminary Proposal", *Law and Contemporary Problems*, Vol. 59, No. 4, 1997.

9 It is worth noting that the National Pact, which brought about the Peace of Timbuktu in northern Mali, also had provision for a TRC. The Malian TRC was never created. Even as it was being negotiated, the rebel team were saying privately that they had no desire whatever to sit in judgement either over their rebel movements, or over the army (personal communication with the authors of *A Peace of Timbuktu*).

10 Hizkias Assefa, op. cit.

ACRONYMS

AFRC	Armed Forces Revolutionary Council
APC	All People's Congress
BBC	British Broadcasting Corporation
CBO	Community-based organization
CDF	Civil Defence Forces
CGG	Campaign for Good Governance
CSO	Civil society organization
CWPDTF	Commonwealth Police Development Task Force
DCR	Disarmament and Conflict Resolution
DDR	Disarmament, demobilization and reintegration
DfID	Department for International Development (United Kingdom)
ECOMOG	ECOWAS Monitoring Group
ECOWAS	Economic Community of West African States
FAWE	Forum for African Women Educationalists
ISU	Internal Security Unit
Le	Leone (Sierra Leone's national currency)
MRU	Mano River Union
MUP	Movement to Unite People
NCC	National Consultative Conference
NCDDR	National Committee for Disarmament, Demobilization and Reintegration
NCDHR	National Commission for Democracy and Human Rights
NCRRR	National Commission for Reconstruction, Resettlement and Rehabilitation
NGO	Non-governmental organization
NPFL	National Patriotic Front of Liberia
NPRC	National Provisional Ruling Council
OAU	Organization of African Unity (now African Union)
PCASED	Programme for Coordination and Assistance for Security and Development
RUF	Revolutionary United Front
RUF/SL	Revolution United Front/Sierra Leone
SLA	Sierra Leone Army
SLPF	Sierra Leone Police Force

SLPP	Sierra Leone People's Party
SSD	Special Security Division
TRC	Truth and Reconciliation Commission
TSA	Transitional Safety Allowances
UDP	United Democratic Party
UFV	United Front Volunteers
UN	United Nations
UNAMSIL	United Nations Mission in Sierra Leone
UNDP	United Nations Development Programme
UNIDIR	United Nations Institute for Disarmament Research
UNOMSIL	United Nations Observer Mission in Sierra Leone